D0074805

MERCYHURST COLLEGE LIBRARY
ERIE, PA.   16546

Silence and Narrative

**Recent Titles in
Contributions in Women's Studies**

Silence and Narrative

The Early Novels
of Gertrude Stein

JANICE L. DOANE

Contributions in Women's Studies, Number 62

Greenwood Press
Westport, Connecticut • London, England

Library of Congress Cataloging-in-Publication Data

Doane, Janice L.
  Silence and narrative.

  (Contributions in women's studies, ISSN 0147-104X ; no. 62)
  Bibliography: p.
  Includes index.
  1. Stein, Gertrude, 1874–1946—Criticism and
interpretation. I. Title. II. Series.
PS3537.T323Z587   1986   813'.52   85-9854
ISBN 0-313-24936-9 (lib. bdg. : alk. paper)

Copyright © 1986 by Janice L. Doane

All rights reserved. No portion of this book may be
reproduced, by any process or technique, without the express written
consent of the publisher.

Library of Congress Catalog Card Number: 85-9854
ISBN: 0-313-24936-9
ISSN: 0147-104X

First published in 1986

Greenwood Press
A division of Congressional Information Service, Inc.
88 Post Road West
Westport, Connecticut 06881

Printed in the United States of America

(∞)™

The paper used in this book complies with the
Permanent Paper Standard issued by the National
Information Standards Organization (Z39.48-1984).

10 9 8 7 6 5 4 3 2 1

Copyright Acknowledgments

Quotations from *Fernhurst, Q.E.D.,* and *Other Early Writings* by Gertrude
Stein are used with the permission of Liveright Publishing Corporation.
Copyright © 1971 by Daniel C. Joseph, Administrator of the Estate of
Gertrude Stein. *Q.E.D.* copyright 1950 by Alice B. Toklas.

Quotations from *Three Lives,* by Gertrude Stein are used with the
permission of Random House, Inc.

Every reasonable effort has been made to trace the owners of copyright
materials used in this book, but in some instances this has proven
impossible. The publishers will be glad to receive information leading to
more complete acknowledgments in subsequent prints of this book and in
the meantime extend their apologies for any omissions.

For my parents,
Mary R. and Ivan G. Doane

Contents

Acknowledgments

I am grateful to many people for their guidance and support. Neil Schmitz encouraged my interest in Gertrude Stein, and his own work on Stein has been a vital inspiration. Murray M. Schwartz, William Warner, and Henry Sussman sharpened my understanding of contemporary critical theory, offered important suggestions for revisions after carefully reading my manuscript, and were always available for much good "talking and listening."

A special word of thanks to: Dianne Hunter, who brought a strong interest in Stein and knowledge of feminist critical theory to bear in her careful readings of my manuscript; to the women of the Buffalo writing group, and to Devon Hodges, and Barb Porter, for reading portions of this manuscript, and for their steady encouragement and support.

My deep gratitude to my parents, for their unwavering interest and faith in all my work, to my husband Jim Mott, whose conviction that my work is valuable has kept me going, to my daughter Sara, for helping me keep everything in perspective.

A grant from the S.U.N.Y. at Buffalo Graduate Student Association enabled me to study Gertrude Stein's manuscripts at Beinecke Library, Yale. A S.U.N.Y. Intercampus Fellowship gave me a year of financial support for uninterrupted writing, partly accomplished at C.U.N.Y. Graduate Center in New York City. I am grateful for both.

Introduction: Silences

Bee time vine be vine truth devine truth.
(Gertrude Stein, *Bee Time Vine*)

At the end of Gertrude Stein's first completed novel, the character Adele delivers a passionate farewell lecture to her lover, Helen: "You are wrong in your theory of the whole duty of silence," Adele insists. "Nothing is too good or holy for clear thinking and definite expression."[1] If Adele is simply taken as a spokeswoman for Stein's ideas, as she generally is, then her comments become ironic when set next to Stein's later difficult and obscure writings. "My writing is clear as mud," Stein cheerfully admitted toward the end of her career, "but mud settles and clear streams run on and disappear."[2] Stein adopted this defensive posture in response to the hostile ridicule her writings inspired. Just ten years after *Q.E.D.* was written, however, Adele's denial of silence and advocacy of clear expression are more subtly qualified in Stein's writings. In the "Rooms" section of *Tender Buttons* the issue of silence is raised in the form of questions: "Why is there that sensible silence.... Does silence choke speech or does it not."[3] These questions are not answered, but Stein again discusses silence in a series of meditations written in 1913 entitled "France" and "England," and in a play, *What Happened*. These short prose pieces, written in the labyrinthine style of *Tender Buttons*, are more concerned with programmatic statements about writing than with the description of France, England, or what happened.

A silence is no more than occasional. It respects understanding and salt and even a rope. ("France")

Silence which makes silence gives that sense to all there is, silence which has light and water and vision and appetite and result and a motion and more exaggeration and no recklessness, silence which is there is not disturbed by expression.

What comes out of silence. What comes out of silence is that which having that usefulness, that nature and that fashion is not shown to be managed by the combination.

Surely silence is sustained and the change is sudden. ("England")

Silence is so windowful. ("What Happened")[4]

Stein's use of the word "silence" deserves close scrutiny. However, for the moment, I would like to focus on her change in tone and attitude. From a vehement denial of silence and an ardent demand for clarity in *Q.E.D.*, Stein moves through a more thoughtful deliberation on silence to a celebration of it, by means of a style that in and of itself is not easily "heard." Silence, in these programmatic-sounding statements, becomes both a metaphoric strategy and an explicit theme. Stein develops not only an appreciation but an aesthetics of silence. What did she find in silence that was "so windowful?" Why did she move from the "audibility" of the realistic novel to the inaudibility of her later experimental style? My purpose in this study is to trace Stein's preoccupation with, and changing attitude toward silence in her early career, in order to understand how and why she developed her silent aesthetic.

In the following chapters I do a close reading of Stein's first four novels: *Q.E.D.*, *Fernhurst*, *Three Lives*, and *The Making of Americans*, a book that prepares us to appreciate the complexity of her mid-career. Stein's first two completed novels, *Q.E.D.* and *Fernhurst*, have only recently emerged from silence. In 1971 Liveright published the original texts of these novels for the first time in a volume that includes Stein's initial attempt to write *The Making of Americans* as well. So far, these narratives have inspired very little critical commentary, though they are of obvious importance in terms of understanding Stein's artistic development. Of the few critics who do address the issues raised by her first two novels, moreover, most remain more attentive to them as autobiographical statements than as literary works.

However, I am more interested in how silence functions in these novels than in simply speaking Stein's silences. Stein herself attempted to preserve the silence of these two texts, most blatantly by deliberately suppressing their publication. Her explicitly voiced reasoning was that they were "too outspoken."[5] That she silenced these "outspoken" texts did not mean that she was entirely unwilling to allow them to speak. Stein's analysis of a lesbian affair in *Q.E.D.* is rendered again in *Fernhurst* by doubling and splitting it into the analysis of one homosexual and one heterosexual affair, and rendered again in *Three Lives*, which she actively tried to publish, as the analysis of numerous "platonic" relationships among women and the heterosexual relationship between Jeff and Melanctha. Her silenced novel, *Fernhurst*, moreover, emerges finally in *The Making of Americans*, though effectively muted by and buried beneath that book's hyperbolic verbiage. Silence, of course, raises the vital issue of censorship and propriety, of what we are allowed to say. But Stein's early novels are not only altered by the attempt to disguise the tabooed content of a lesbian affair. Each time Stein rewrites her affair, she does so from a different position, one that becomes more and more complicit with Helen's position and the silence Adele castigated so firmly. Stein's preoccupation with this silence, and her growing desire to in some way preserve it, puts pressure upon conventional narrative requirements. In *The Making of Americans* she talked herself out of speaking by means of these requirements entirely, which has meant that she also talked most people out of giving her a hearing. Having found her own voice, Stein became, in effect, silent. This silence however, was not simply a necessity but an artistic choice.

In order to appreciate this choice, one familiar understanding of the literary strategy of silence needs to be revised. The artist's concern with silence is often read as an other-worldly gesture, as the attempt to attain or represent the eternal, or a

mystical realm beyond language. This definition would feed
into the overly familiar, but not particularly enlightening, image of Stein as an oracle or sibyl, or as an immobile and con-
templative Buddha, an image made popular by the many
carefully posed sculptures, paintings, and photographs of her.
Stein, of course, did not discourage this rather seductive image
of herself, but when it came to her writings, talk about mys-
ticism was angrily denounced as "rot."[6] Stein did love to write
about and contemplate eternity, but only toward the end of her
career. In her early career, her preoccupation with silence meant
a more worldly concern with what she could say and how she
could speak.

Thus, silence is not simply an absence—from language or
from this world. In Stein's early novels, silence is a very felt
presence, as can be demonstrated simply by the bulk of her
first two novels alone. *Q.E.D.*, where silence is given a great
deal of play, is twice as long as *Fernhurst*, where Stein's interest
in silence is suppressed and speech is seen as a moral imperative. Stein's interest in silence hardly meant that she began
to subtract things, as Michael Hoffman claims in his study,
The Development of Abstractionism. Hoffman sees the development of Stein's aesthetic as simply the *subtraction* of "traditional narrative elements" from her prose. I will demonstrate
that Stein's developing aesthetic presents us with more of a
paradox than this. Her prose became increasingly difficult and
silent as she forced these "traditional narrative elements" into
view by stylizing, and making them excessive, thus insisting
upon and exposing the very elements the novelist is ordinarily
required to keep discreet and subdued. Her increasing interest
in silence did not mean the subtraction of anything. Rather, it
meant the attempt to find a decentered authorial mode that
would allow her to include more—to bring in and give equal
respect and attention to what she calls "the surrounding extra"
in *Tender Buttons*—such trivia as "salt and even a rope." "All
along the tendency to deplore the absence of more has not been
authorized," she points out in *Tender Buttons.*[7]

Silence haunts all writing and speech, but many writers have
considered its possibilities as a manifest mode of authority.
Kierkegaard, for example, insisted upon "indirect communi-

cation," and invented the pseudonym "Johannes de Silentio" for his author of *Fear and Trembling*. Kierkegaard's exploration of narrative strategies aligns him with many modernists for whom silence was also an explicit concern. Henry James, whom Hugh Kenner describes as "flushed with orgies of reticence,"[8] became increasingly obsessed, especially in his later works, with "not telling." Joyce's young artist in *A Portrait* vows "silence, exile, and cunning." Beckett's narrator in *The Unnamable* is involved in a Sisyphean struggle to go on speaking: "All words, there's nothing else, you must go on, that's all I know, they're going to stop, I know that well, I can feel it, they're going to abandon me, it will be the silence for a moment, a good few moments."[9] If silence sometimes implicated these modernists in failure or exhaustion, Stein's phrase "silence is so windowful" is obviously lyrical, even celebratory. Besides the pun on wonderful, "windowful" also suggests a room full of windows, of many different perspectives, or, more ironically, that Stein felt she was achieving, for all her "muddy prose," a certain clarity and even transparency. If, on one level, Stein saw her silent aesthetic as offering the same possibilities as a more literal silence—the opportunity to contemplate or give play to a variety of different perspectives, this particular attitude was shared by other modernists who violated a single point of view, notably William Faulkner and Virginia Woolf, especially in her novel *The Waves*. On the most general level, the preoccupation with silence informed an experimental strategy. Of all periods of literary history, modernism, with its emphasis upon radical innovation, most consistently valorized the transgression of our familiar categories of discourse, and hence, our understanding.

Susan Sontag exemplifies a common attitude toward these transgressions in her essay on modernism, "The Aesthetics of Silence." Sontag includes Gertrude Stein in a group of twentieth-century writers whom Sontag claims transgressed in order to transcend. The modern artist, according to Sontag, was engaged in a "spiritual" conflict with the material forms of his art—the very concreteness, mediacy, and historicity of words—which he comes to perceive as a "trap." Faced with the possibility of sacrificing his vision either to the "treachery of words" or to the peanut-crunching crowd of consumers, patrons, and clients who would distort it, the twentieth-century artist consistently chose to "purify" himself by silence—either by choosing to forsake his art altogether, as did Rimbaud and Wittgenstein, or to go on writing but to stop communicating. In the first instance, the artist believed that his "permanent silence" guaranteed him a "certificate of unchallengeable seriousness." In the latter instance, the artist chose a "contradictory form of silence": he goes on speaking but in a way that is inaccessible to his hearers. For Sontag, this act essentially amounts to an act of bad faith. The audience is reduced to a group of "voyeuristic spectators," forced to "stare" at this opaque writing as at a blank wall. The writer's silence is an offensive weapon, according to Sontag, who characterizes the modern artist as aggressive, and even "sadistic." [10]

Sontag is certainly not the only critic of modernism to have leveled accusations of incomprehensibility and bad faith at twentieth-century writers. In her polemic, we can hear the echo of familiar and still tenacious critical attitudes toward Stein. Was Stein a "fraud" who simply perpetrated a very bad joke? How seriously can we take her? In all probability, Stein was seriously joking,[11] but Stein's seriousness is always an explicit and important issue for her critics, who resolve to move "cautiously" in their assessment of her. Michael Hoffman designates this group the "dispassionate" critics. Counting himself among them, Hoffman claims that these critics negotiate the extreme poles of early reaction to Stein—ardent admiration or blind hostility, both provoked by a personal knowledge of her— by adopting a more objective attitude, a goal to be more easily achieved, he claims, because these critics do not base their assessment on a personal knowledge of Stein or an attitude toward her life.[12]

However, taking Stein seriously is hardly a goal to be achieved simply by the resolve to be serious and dispassionate. Richard Bridgman, for example, whom Hoffman includes in his group of "dispassionate critics," and who is perhaps her most influential critic, reveals his resolve to take Stein seriously by claiming that he is more concerned with writing a "description of her works" than a description of her life, and, if nothing else, by the ambitious nature of his task, which is to carefully survey the whole of Stein's career. Yet, Bridgman can barely suppress his disdain either for Stein's prose or for what he clearly perceives to be her excessive emotional life. Stein borders perilously close to hysteria in Bridgman's account of her early career. Overtaken by emotions she could barely control, "she permitted her feelings to spill messily onto the pages of her college themes";[13] her early novels, Bridgman claims, are records of her fluctuating and overwhelming psychological life. Bridgman often makes useful and interesting observations about the development of Stein's style, but these observations are most often closed off by his more attentive focus on the nature of this psychological life. Thus, without careful explanation of what he feels to be the formal requirements of the novel as a genre, or how and why Stein violates these requirements, Bridgman simply pronounces *The Making of Americans* to be "disastrous as a novel," but of personal value to Stein as a way of "purging her psyche of old ghosts" and as "a psychological and stylistic daybook."[14] Stein's experimentation and contributions to literature are then the outcome of her energy and emotional life, which do not, however, inform a sustained intellectual inquiry. Rather, from Bridgman's account of her early career Stein emerges as an elephantess in the china shop of literature: "Expending prodigious amounts of energy, Stein thrashed erratically toward innovation."[15]

By contrast, Wendy Steiner, who has written more recently on Stein, studies Stein's "portraits" both by placing them in a larger context of portraiture as a genre of literature and painting, and by reading these portraits as a programmatic, self-conscious enterprise. Yet, the question of whether or not to apologize for Stein is still a vital issue and explicit concern. "What this book is not, is an apology for Stein,"[16] Steiner announces at the beginning of her book. Steiner hardly means that she is about to blindly advocate Stein's writing, but that she, like the "dispassionate critics," aims at a balanced view, aware of, and willing to concede all of Stein's shortcomings and nonsense. Thus her refusal to apologize essentially amounts to an apology, for when we apologize we admit and ask forgiveness for an error or transgression against propriety. An apology restores harmony and allows two discordant groups to go on speaking to each other. One would hardly think of apologizing or not apologizing for James Joyce, who has been granted his certificate of seriousness and place in the literary canon. That Stein's literary reputation is still haunted by the issue of apology indicates that she transgressed the limits of literary propriety more radically than any other modernist. Of all the "silent" writers Sontag mentions, Stein still remains the most silent of all.

That Steiner can be seen as apologizing even when she claims she is not, and that one of the "dispassionate critics" has an obviously disdainful attitude toward Stein, raises the question of whether gestures of apology and claims of disinterest are useful critical gestures. Steiner's statement is revealing, but it does not add to or subtract from her rigorous and valuable study. More importantly, the pose of objective observer who simply "writes descriptions" has been put into question by modern writers in general, and Stein very specifically.

Stein, like her critics, was concerned with explanations, and her early novels are a passionately conducted search for truth. As Michel Foucault points out in his "Discourse on Language," it is under the impetus of the "will to truth" that what he calls a "true discourse" has been formulated. Historically constituted in classical Greek thought, true discourse contributed in "the sixteenth and seventeenth centuries to the will to knowledge, which sketched out a schema of possible, observable, measurable, and classifiable objects and imposed upon the knowing subject a certain *position*, a certain *viewpoint* and a certain *function*."[17] This schema has imposed itself upon other forms of discourse. For example, Foucault points out the ways in which "Western literature has for centuries sought to base itself in nature, in the plausible, upon science and sincerity— in short, upon true discourse."[18] In literary criticism, gestures toward apology, and claims of disinterest, meant to establish both our credibility and Stein's plausibility, indicate that we too operate within the constraints of true discourse. If Stein, as William Gass rightfully notes, used "self-protective language" in her early career, so too, as Gass further notes, do her critics.[19] Stein raises these issues so explicitly because she was so explicitly concerned with them herself, and because she so radically transgressed the constraints of true discourse. Stein questions our most cherished assumptions of how meaning and truth are established; yet both Sontag and Bridgman reveal that they do not understand this project before they adopt an attitude toward it.

Sontag's categories of understanding and explanation are a familiar set of dualisms: self/other, spirit/matter (soul/body), silence/speech. According to Sontag, these realms confront the artist with an either-or choice. The artist can choose either the spiritual or the material, "permanent silence" or speech, his/her vision and self, or the audience, the other. If the artist chooses silence within speech, his or her choice is "contradictory." Sontag can view this choice as contradictory only because she keeps her terms distinctly separate and opposed. One of these poles, moreover, is inevitably privileged in Sontag's polemic, while the other is condemned, thus allowing and encouraging her own vehemence. Most twentieth-century writers and thinkers, on the other hand, have collapsed these familiar oppositions. Sigmund Freud's discovery of the unconscious, for example, revealed the other within the self, a permanent silence which yet speaks through bodily symptoms and acting out. Jacques Derrida subverts the hierarchization of these oppositions by his concept of "*differance*," and demonstrates the way in which each term in the familiar binary oppositions of Western metaphysics is actually the accomplice of the other. Writing within this tradition, Michel Foucault discusses silence as integral to speech:

Silence itself—the things one declines to say, or is forbidden to name, the discretion that is required between different speakers—is less the absolute limit of discourse, the other side from which it is separated by a strict boundary, than an element that functions alongside the things said, with them and in relation to them within over-all strategies. There is no binary division to be made between what one says and what one does not say; we must try to determine the different ways of not saying such things, how those who can and those who cannot speak of them are distributed, which type of discourse is authorized, or which form of discretion is required in either case. There are not one but many silences, and they are an integral part of the strategies that underlie and permeate discourses.[20]

Sontag is not obliged, of course, to agree with the analysis of these twentieth-century thinkers. She does, however, discuss the way in which twentieth-century writers sabotage the traditional patterns of reading that establish hierarchy, but because she does not consider the nature of the implicit epistemological project, she renders this strategy superfluous and even aggressive.

Her assumption that the writer is deliberately aggressive, however, arises from a *non sequitur*: if the artist is inaccessible, he doesn't want to communicate. She does not take into account, as Henry James did, for example, in *The Wings of the Dove*, that silence can arise "not from ill-will . . . but from a failure of common terms."[21] Sontag assumes that communication can be unproblematic, without considering the terms on which such an ideally unproblematic language would be based. Instead, she considers language to be clear or not clear, and believes in a level of language that is transparent, neutral, and innocent. This is the assumption, par excellence, of nineteenth-century realism, a century and philosophy that Sontag's ultimately conservative essay would send us scurrying back to for refuge. Sontag's conservatism is somewhat surprising, since she has expressed her interest in modernism in other ways, especially by introducing the controversial theorist of modernism, Roland Barthes, to this country. Incomprehensibility is so threatening, as Stein understood, because the creation of meaning is so vital to our existence. Incomprehensibility, however, is too often experienced as meaninglessness. Stein ultimately came to perceive the "impossibility" of meaninglessness, a word that could be seen as simply a catch-all for the mind's desire for stasis. An active mind, she was sure, would always search for ways to create meaning.[22] It would be more appropriate, then, to view her transgressions against the requirements that establish truth and meaning, not as attempts to befuddle us with "meaninglessness," but as attempts to provoke us to create meaning in a new way.

Bridgman also preserves a still tenacious binary division,

and how to speak the truth is the issue implicit in his choice
of title. As his epigraph indicates, Bridgman takes his title,
Gertrude Stein in Pieces, from one of Stein's own questions:
"Why don't you speak in pieces and say no matter." Bridgman
does not discuss his reasons for choosing this epigraph, but it
was obviously not one of them to confront the issue of unity
that Stein's question poses and challenges. Unity is one of our
most tenacious requirements in the production of meaning and
truth. In the narrative, unity is secured by repetitive elements,
which establish its theme, and the traditional structure of beginning, middle, and ending. Why Stein found it necessary to
transgress these requirements is obviously a vital question.
However, instead of addressing this question by putting it in
the context of a general twentieth-century movement that has
subverted unity by increasing fragmentation, or even addressing the nature of Stein's dissatisfaction with narrative requirements, Bridgman takes an easier route. It was Stein herself
who was "in pieces"; therefore, so was her prose.

Reading a woman's writings as simply a personal statement
or as the barometer of her emotional life is not an uncommon
strategy. Bridgman obsessively locks Stein into the realm of
the personal and emotional, effectively silencing her critique
of larger contexts. Thus, Bridgman claims, Stein read Aristotle
only for what she could glean from him to resolve her own
personal conflicts.[23] The anxious attempt to maintain the dichotomy male/female relies upon assigning each position in
this dichotomy a certain meaning and then preserving the integrity of this position by insisting upon the integrity of that
meaning. Thus some feminists insist upon the integrity of the
personal and emotional, while Bridgman insists upon the integrity of the intellectual, preserving his own integrity, moreover, by leaving a woman in pieces. Bridgman reveals his own
chauvinism by more than one "descriptive image" meant to
help us negotiate Stein's difficult prose. Responding, perhaps
unconsciously, to the theme of matriarchy in *The Making of
Americans* that he points out but does not investigate, Bridgman compares that book to "a great sow surrounded by suck-
lings" (her portraits). Bridgman's engagement with Stein's prose
is qualified by an unacknowledged bias that forces him to hold

his nose. Offering another analogy, Bridgman compares the narration of that book to the "bumps, lurches, wild wrenchings of the wheel, and sudden brakings" of someone learning to drive, evoking the cliché of women both as bad drivers and forever-amateur writers. Bridgman's nasty witticisms, emerging sharply from his otherwise judicious prose, especially in his chapter on *The Making of Americans*, indicate that he feels increasingly threatened as Stein's writings become more discomposed and discomposing. Instead of resorting to "great sows" and old saws for comfort, we should more carefully consider Stein's position as a woman writer, and the way in which this position informed her radical transgressions.[24] Stein herself perceived her position as a woman writer to be an important consideration, whether or not we agree with the unladylike boast in which she posed the question. "Why is it," she asked in *The Geographical History of America*, "that in this epoch the only real literary thinking has been done by a woman?"[25]

Stein's life and writings do not allow us to ascribe an implicit essentialism to her question: women have certain inherent qualities that better qualified Stein for some "real literary thinking." Stein, as just about everyone knows, hardly privileged the "feminine" and did not always like to think of herself as a woman. In *Q.E.D.*, Stein's surrogate, Adele, appropriates a male pose and voice, and proclaims from this position: "I always did thank God I was not born a woman."[26] Stein has provoked scandal by calling the "facts" of the biological categories of sexuality into question, not simply in her life but also in her writings. Even so, she could not escape, as is obvious from Bridgman's account, being judged by the assumptions based upon these categories. Indeed, Stein initially shared these assumptions, even as she began to challenge them.

An exploration of Stein's silences raises one of the issues crucial to feminist literary criticism: how can women speak with authority in a patriarchal culture? To answer this question, I am advocating that we be attentive to the analysis of discourse provided by contemporary theorists.[27] At stake is not simply "speech" but our desire to be speakers of truth and creators of meaning, and to be heard as such. This involves, as Foucault observes in his "Discourse on Language," that we consider the requirements of the discourse available to us. "It is always possible," Foucault remarks, "that one could speak the truth in a void; one would only be in the true (i.e., heard), however, if one obeyed the discursive 'policy' which would have to be reactivated every time one spoke."[28] The first requirement of this "discursive 'policy'" has long been the valorization of a male voice and position. As current feminists have amply demonstrated, if anyone's voice has been stifled by the "prodigious machinery which propagates true discourse" it is women's, for in the hierarchical operation of the binary divisions which secure truth and meaning, speech has been awarded to the male, silence and negativity to the female. Posited by Western discourse as the negative of the positive, the mirror image of man, "such," writes Josette Feral, "is the non-locus of woman—wanting to be the man that she is not while refusing what she is."[29] Denial of one's "femininity" and identification with what is represented as "masculine", then, was, and is, a common survival technique of women, and puts into perspective Adele's pose and Stein's apparent chauvinism. Stein accepted the viability of the binary division, male/female, with its attendant values, and her beginning premise in *Q.E.D.*'s logical demonstration is that in order to speak, in order to be anywhere at all, she must begin by placing herself as a male speaker.

It is illuminating to explore the effects of this denial—of her position as a woman, and of silence. I say "denial" because if Adele is angry at Helen for not speaking, she is also angry at herself for initially identifying with and enjoying the silences of their relationship, silences that seemed to offer "so many possibilities," and a variety of perspectives from which to interpret the relationship. An exploration of Stein's attraction to silence within her first novel will prepare us for her later interest in it. The power of the logical demonstration, *Q.E.D.*, however, depends upon arriving at a definite position. Adele's anger at the end arises from an insistent attempt to separate herself from Helen in order to maintain her own integrity and identity. Maintaining her integrity and power of speech by means of her chosen masculine pose and position was an uneasy means of survival—the vehemence of her denial indicating the depths of the crisis being repressed. The progression of Stein's novels does not reveal an increasing ease with speech or traditional literary authority; instead it reflects an increasing sensitivity to the effects of this repression, and the requirements that maintain it. In *Fernhurst*, Stein picks up where she left off in *Q.E.D.*, but with an even more adamant insistence upon a definite position which relies for its power upon a diatribe against feminism and women.

I consider this conflict, again, not simply as Stein's personal, emotional crisis, but as a replay, if exaggerated, of a crisis that comes from cultural positioning, and the narrative conventions that not only generate but sustain this crisis. I would agree, then, with Jean Kennard, who calls for a feminist reading that would emphasize the study of narrative structure, and the very way in which women are "victimized" by its conventions.[30] Kennard selects for analysis one particular convention—of the "two suitors"—that inevitably privileges the male. As we shall see, Stein, too, demonstrates the disastrous effects of a conventional plot, which in "Lena," for example, leaves a woman not only devastated but dead, while her mate, roughly of the same caliber, is encouraged and left to contentedly carry on. In a framework where the male is privileged and the female is powerless, women are more vulnerable to these "plots" and women writers more apt to be in conflict with them. Because the male is privileged by these conventions, women will have less of a stake in their perpetuation. However, the scope of Stein's transgressions prompts me to work on a more generalized level than Kennard. Men can be victims of these conventions as well. Thus, in *The Making of Americans*, Stein transgressed the requirements of literary characterization in order to formulate the characters of both men and women in a new way.

In this respect, the conventional conclusion of the nineteenth-century novel secures not only the unity of the story, and thus the integrity of the narrator, but, as Leo Bersani has pointed out, the repression or immobilization of desire.[31] In *Q.E.D.*, Adele renounces her desire for Helen and concedes to her rival Mabel, in the interest of attaining her own identity and integrity. And yet, though she had denounced this rival and attempted to silence her, she must borrow from and identify with her strategies. The triangular affair of *Q.E.D.* has all the configurations of an oedipal drama, which is not surprising, since as modern theorists have observed, narrative teleology re-enacts the oedipal drama, and its momentum is generated by the search for the father's name and authority. Stein makes this family configuration the explicit configuration of her own narrative in *Fernhurst* by the genealogical placement of her characters. However, the person who is vested with this authority in *Fernhurst* is not a man, but a woman, Miss Thornton.

Stein's novels, as several readers have pointed out, rarely have any male characters in them. Again, this does not mean that male positions are not represented. Stein's novels reveal all the ways women have of speaking and not speaking in a literary framework and culture that privilege the male voice and position. There are several options: women can become entirely silent and passive objects of rivalry, like Helen and her representatives—Janet Bruce in *Fernhurst*, Lena in *Three Lives*—or they are given the option of speaking by either appropriating or speaking for male authority—Adele and Mabel in *Q.E.D.*, Miss Thornton in *Fernhurst*, Rose in "Melanctha," Aunt Mathilda in "Lena." Miss Thornton is caught in the bind, however, of speaking for women by means of the very rules of propriety that have been used to oppress them. This conflict is intensified and made more explicit by the Good Anna, who has so thoroughly internalized the requirements of the propriety of servants and "good girls" that her conflicting desire to speak with authority and be the master renders her self-destructive. The other option for women in Stein's novels is to be silent speakers—those who subvert the father's authority by pleasing, coaxing and flattering him into accepting their plans—or those who very simply go on speaking even if no one is listening, as does Mrs. Dehning in *The Making of Americans*. In *Three Lives* and *The Making of Americans*, Stein increasingly identifies with positions of silence, of hesitancy in speaking, as is evident most obviously by the way in which her narrator adopts the "inarticulate" dialect of the servants whose lives she renders. However, *Three Lives* reveals an intensified conflict: even as Stein becomes more hesitant she also becomes more insistent. Thus, Stein stylizes repetition, the narrative requirement that secures the unity and integrity of any narrative by binding beginning and ending, and makes excessive, and therefore manifest, a narrative element that is usually kept discreet. Stein ultimately saw the requirements that secure unity and integrity in both narratives and the life they recount as especially oppressive in their formulation of the woman's character, for they insist upon the immobilization of her disruptive desire, her goodness, her passivity, and often, her death.

Stein both writes about and stylizes beginnings in *The Making of Americans*, a book that makes her previously implicit quest for identity explicit by investigating her own family's history—their move from the Old World to the New. Beginning her family's history not with its patriarchs but with its matriarchs, she gradually evolves in this monstrous book a system of knowing and understanding everyone "who is or ever has been living" that deliberately attempts to include and define the "existences" of women. Her attempt to compose everyone's existences, however, is complicated by her increasing hesitance to speak for others, of importance in *Three Lives*, and emerging in this book even more clearly. To get it right, to include more— of what she had excluded or previously neglected, and of the perspectives of silent contemplation—Stein stylizes the beginning, and by beginning again and again, she differs from her previous conclusions and thus defers an ultimate one. Consequently, the novel's unity, and the concept of identity, its traditional quest, have been put so far into question that her novel is one of the most "illiterate" ever written. Having begun her career in the name of the father, Stein ends this book by considering the possibilities of "illegitimacy," of a different mode of authority.

I am claiming then, that by exploiting the subversive potential of the silences that haunt her early texts, Stein begins to develop a mode of authority that deliberately challenges what she later called "patriarchal poetry." But if Stein increasingly puts into question her own initial assumption of a male pose, it is not in order to discover an exclusively "female discourse," if this in fact would be possible. Simply by assuming a male pose in the beginning, Stein put into question the dichotomous oppositions she initially believed. As she does so more self-consciously, other requirements that traditionally secure truth, the father's name, a divine origin, are transgressed, displaced, replaced. Truth is not divine, but devined, set free from its old support system. In this endeavor, Stein was joined by other modernists, who, however, transgressed these requirements for other reasons. As a woman with little stake in the system that hardly gave her an equal voice, and generated such conflicts for her, Stein transgressed more radically. But her alternative mode of discourse cannot simply be valorized as speech, for learning to speak it was integrally bound up with an appreciation of silence. By beginning the story again to include more, perhaps we can gain a better understanding of this and other of Stein's silences.

I

Identity, Silence, and the Echo of Desire in *Q.E.D.*

He had not the strength to take irony's vow of silence, not the power to keep it; and only the man who keeps silent amounts to anything... He who knows how to keep silent discovers an alphabet which has just as many letters as the one commonly in use. (Kierkegaard)
Silence is so windowful (Gertrude Stein)

I. A Story of Publication

Speaking to a friend about *Q.E.D.*, Gertrude Stein once described that novel as "too outspoken for the times, even though it was restrained."[1] And being "too outspoken" her first completed novel remained silent, buried beneath a gradually accumulating pile of later manuscripts, unpublished until after its author's death. Stein was referring in that conversation to the novel's subject matter, a lesbian relationship. Her discretion seems reasonable if we keep in mind the court battles waged over the censorship of such "uninhibited" modern texts as *Ulysses*, *Lady Chatterley's Lover*, and *The Well of Loneliness*. There were other considerations demanding her tact as well. As Leon Katz has shown, the novel is a fairly explicit record of an affair Stein became involved in while a medical student at Johns Hopkins. The novel's characters—Adele, Mabel Neathe, and Helen Thompson—would have been easily recognizable in their "real-life" counterparts—Stein, Mabel Haynes and May Bookstaver.[2] Stein's later relationship with Alice B. Toklas demanded protection as well.

Perhaps, then, for all of these reasons, the route to publication took a more deflected course for *Q.E.D.* than for the modern novels mentioned above. It gets its first, unnamed and shadowy mention with the publication of *The Autobiography of Alice B. Toklas*. There, Stein has her narrator, Alice, tell us that Gertrude claimed to have forgotten the novel, and came across it only accidentally thirty years after it was written:

> The funny thing about this short novel is that she completely forgot about it for many years. She remembered herself beginning a little later writing the Three Lives but this first piece of writing was completely forgotten, she had never mentioned it to me, even when I first knew her. She must have forgotten about it almost immediately.[3]

We could claim that this statement is simply untrue. The plot of the lesbian relationship of *Q.E.D.* is transformed, almost point by point, into the plot of the heterosexual relationship of the "Melanctha" story in *Three Lives*, published in 1909. And so, in a manner of speaking, *Q.E.D.* was first published in the guise of "Melanctha." However, to take Stein's claim in the *Autobiography* at face value, we ourselves would have to forget not only that the complex question of the truth of memory is at issue in the *Autobiography*, but also that the play with the fusion and confusion of identities is the very mainspring of that book. Stein remained sympathetically loyal to Toklas's feelings by not publishing *Q.E.D.* The nature of Toklas's involvement with the publication of that novel suggest what those feelings were.

Alice was still jealous enough of Gertrude's previous relationship to May Bookstaver to burn all of May's letters in 1932.[4] After Gertrude had found the manuscript of *Q.E.D.* she gave Alice both the manuscript and the choice about its publication. In 1947, Alice's sensitivity and discretion were still getting the better part of her valor. Loyal to Gertrude's will which requested the publication of all her manuscripts, Alice nonetheless admitted to "cowardice" in the face of that task in a letter to a friend:

It is a subject I haven't known how to handle nor known from what point to act upon. It was something I knew I'd have to meet some day and not too long hence and to cover my cowardice I kept saying—well when everything else is accomplished.

Alice adds that she would not want the book published while she is alive. "Gertrude would have understood this perfectly though of course it was never mentioned."[5]

Alice managed both to overcome her scruples and to safeguard them. She eventually published the novel in 1950 in an edition of 516 copies, thereby fulfilling Gertrude's request for publication but limiting the book's accessibility. Along with a few minor changes of the text, the novel appeared with an ironically apt new title, *Things As They Are.*

With a view toward telling us how things really were, Leon Katz has written an introduction to a new edition of *Q.E.D.*, published by Liveright in 1971. This edition not only makes the novel generally accessible for the first time, but also restores the book to its original text and title. The text is framed for us by Katz's introduction which provides an account of the love affair upon which Stein's novel was based. According to Katz, Stein simply "wrote out the whole story literally as it happened" and therefore the love affair is "recounted in minute and accurate detail" in *Q.E.D.*[6]

Relying most heavily upon *Q.E.D.*, but with the additional help of letters, interviews, and Stein's early manuscripts, Katz only mildly corrects the image of Stein as she had projected it into her character Adele. According to Katz, as a student at Hopkins, Gertrude joined her brother Leo in a crusade to reform the morals of their Baltimore circle of friends. Leo was successful while Gertrude was heavy-handed in her emulation of him. Stein accused others of "raw virginity" while suffering from it herself, and attempted to "bludgeon" and "sandbag" her friends out of their bourgeois moral torpor. Her frontal attack was inadequate to the more sophisticated ploys of social intercourse, which her friends understood but she did not. Her "assertive naivete" came to an end, however, in the years of her involvement with May which provided her with her "first instruction in genuine passion." Although it was a difficult lesson for Stein, who was mildly repulsed, tortured by self doubts and doubts about May's feelings, she allowed herself to "drift in the ambiguity" of her feelings. The turning point in the relationship came when Stein put aside the ambiguities of her moral and emotional conflicts and placed herself "into position" in relationship to May and Mabel. Stein's insight at this moment, according to Katz, was that it was not Stein's conflicts but character and personality differences that were bringing the relationship to an impasse. While Stein could see "things as they are," May could not; the relationship ended with a deadlock, and Stein "settled into the pain of frustration for good." Her affair was thus the beginning of her "somber psychological wisdom."[7]

For Katz, this psychological wisdom was based upon the insight of unchangeable character types and differences, the knowledge that the "tangibility of relations did not blur." This insight gave impetus to her later writings which gradually persuade us that what is so is so, and her career culminated in "a vision of the literally true."[8] Katz's version of Stein's career not only echoes the final words of the character Adele in *Q.E.D.*; his version of the love affair and Stein's career as a whole echoes the novel's predictable pattern of the *bildungsroman*.

For this reason it is less important to dismiss either Katz's invaluable research, or his version of Stein's career, than to note the ways in which his methods and conclusions participate in the novel's own conventional assumptions. Granting Katz's assumption that Stein was embarking in the novel upon an attempt at self-representation and the representation of an event in her life, we can note the ways in which that endeavor participates in the variety of displacements which constitute the traditional novel. As J. Hillis Miller points out:

The novel is in various ways a chain of displacements—displacement of its author into the intended role of the narrator, further displacement of the narrator into the lives of imaginary characters . . . displacement of the "origin" of the story (in historical events or in the life experience of the author) into the fictitious events of the narrative.[9]

The assumption which informs these displacements, according to Miller, is the novel's assumption of itself as history. The genre participates in a nineteenth-century notion of history's teleology; its traditional format of beginning, middle and end is a progressive march forward to final fruition in destiny and meaning. Thus, "the assumption that his narrative is history gives more than simply a foundation to the novelist's work," Miller claims. "It also," he writes, quoting a statement of Henry James's, " 'inserts into his attempt a backbone of logic.' "[10] Without this most crucial displacement, then, the displacement of itself onto history and logic, the novel would not only be spineless but "nowhere."[11]

"Q.E.D." is the signature of logic itself, the sign at the end of a geometric proof; perhaps the backbone of this conventional novel is so painfully exposed to view because the assumptions it supported were becoming so emaciated. There would be something mildly pathetic, then, about seeing *Q.E.D.* as relying upon illusive constructs of logic to provide Stein with a notion of her destiny, the "meaning of her life." Pathetic that is, if Stein's novel were not in itself an ironic self-appraisal, that irony guaranteeing an escape from the very assumptions it relies upon. A novel which desperately attempts to put everything in its place, *Q.E.D.* manages to speak its dissatisfaction with the displacements it becomes involved in. In a series of constitutive displacements, irony becomes the displacement of displacements. Irony is the last refuge of the assertive and as such, takes refuge in the very thing it denounces.

We must qualify Katz's assumptions, then, about Adele's character, *Q.E.D.*, and Stein's career as simply an "accurate" recording of the "literally true." *Q.E.D.* is indeed autobiographical. This does not mean, however, that it literally recounts the events of Stein's affair, nor that it gives us a full and transparent picture of her character. In thinking about the relationship between life and autobiography, Paul de Man suggests that we revise our notions of cause and effect:

We assume that life *produces* the autobiography as an act produces its consequences, but can we not suggest, with equal justice, that the autobiographical project may itself produce and determine the life and that whatever the writer *does* is in fact governed by the technical demands of self-portraiture and thus determined, in all its aspects by the resources of the medium?[12]

By beginning her act of self-portraiture and self-exploration within the framework of the realistic novel, Stein had to negotiate the demands of the medium she chose: the displacements of herself onto the narrator, her character Adele, and a temporal, historical progression of event. These demands of the realistic novel produce not a "true" self, but at least a character for the self that is intelligible and coherent. Thus Stein could be pleased and displeased. By producing this coherent statement she could understand herself and her "place" in the affair. But, as we shall see, her ironic attitude in *Q.E.D.* indicates that she was displeased with this definite positioning and coherent formulation as soon as she attained it. Irony was her escape from the necessities of this coherent formulation. Irony allows us to keep something in silence and reserve; it is a counter-statement that has no definite meaning but merely designates the author's absence from his or her explicit statements. These explicit statements are made and allowed to stand—but the author is elsewhere. It is important to be attentive to Stein's ironic attitude immediately, for it is Stein's first strategy, one that pervades her early career, in her lifelong battle against accepting conventional definitions and formulations of the self and identity.

Q.E.D., then, and its history of publication, pose the complexities involved in speaking oneself, and the question not only of what we are allowed to say, but also by what mechanisms we formulate what we do say. Literary statements are never "full" and "transparent"; rather, they are displacements generated by something kept in silence and reserve. Since Freud, we know that displacement is one of the principal strategies of unconscious desire. These displacements or substitutes, generated by the censorship of desire, are destined never to be wholly satisfactory. Thus desire is not erased by censorship, but repeated, disguised, displaced. Desire is repressed by the same agency which images it for us in the manifestations of the dream. Hence, censorship's repressive function becomes more complex because it is both oppressive and creative.

But if all we can know is that manifest content of the text, the effects of dreamwork and not the dream, then the act of interpretation is itself constituted by censorship and the displacements of censorship. While endeavoring to "speak the unspoken" we should understand that this very act is generated by the power of silence, the forgotten, and unconscious desire.

II. A Story of Stories

The women one meets—what are they but books one has already read? You're a whole library of the unknown, the uncut. . . . Upon my word, I've a subscription! (Merton Densher to Kate Croy, *The Wings of the Dove*)

His word is not his own word only, and his Muse has whored with many before him. (Harold Bloom, *Anxiety of Influence*)

Of all Stein's writings, *Q.E.D.* speaks most clearly within the tradition of other literature. The novel echoes narrative conventions and literary ideas Stein had absorbed in the long hours she sat reading through centuries of literature in the British museum in 1902, the year before she completed *Q.E.D.* The several literary allusions of *Q.E.D.* lend a particularly bookish ambiance to the story's passionate affair. These allusions strongly suggest that Stein was not recording her affair in any simple way; certainly, she did not simply transcribe ideas and information about that affair directly from May Bookstaver's letters, as Alice B. Toklas at one point suggested.[13] Though writing the novel may have served Stein as therapy for the pain of defeat and frustration, and as a means of understanding herself in that relationship, recording that affair was also a self-conscious literary exercise. The question of her identity became inextricably interwoven with the complex question of literary identification.

The story of *Q.E.D.* is preceded by an epigraph from Shakespeare's comedy of mistaken identity, *As You Like It*; the quote is selected from a point in the play where three of the characters are speaking for their love. Phebe, a shepherdess, is in love with Ganymede, who is actually Rosalind, the banished daughter of a duke, who has disguised herself as a young man. Orlando is in love with Rosalind and of course does not recognize her in the disguise of Ganymede. Silvius, a shepherd, is in love with Phebe, and is jealous of Ganymede (Rosalind), who has just received a love letter from Phebe. Ganymede, or Rosalind, mocks Phebe's declaration of love and tells her to love Silvius, who is faithful and devoted to her. Thus Rosalind's pose as a young man demands that she speak about herself surreptitiously. Both to maintain the truth and hide it, she speaks by denial, while the others affirm their love:

Phebe: Good shepherd, tell this youth what 'tis to love.

Silvius: It is to be all made of sighs and tears;
      And so am I for Phebe.

Phebe: And I for Ganymede.

Orlando: And I for Rosalind.

Rosalind: And I for no woman.

Silvius: It is to be all made of faith and service;
      And so am I for Phebe.

Phebe: And I for Ganymede.

Orlando: And I for Rosalind.

Rosalind: And I for no woman.

Silvius: It is to be all made of fantasy,
      All made of passion, and all made of wishes;
      All made of adoration, duty and observance;
      All humbleness, all patience, and impatience;
      All purity, all trial, all deservings;
      And so am I for Phebe.

Phebe: And so am I for Ganymede.

Orlando: And so am I for Rosalind.

Rosalind: And so am I for no woman.

Phebe can only take so much confusion. If Rosalind, or Ganymede, can speak for no woman, then how can (s)he blame Phebe for loving him?

Phebe: If this be so, why blame you me to love you?

As if there were an echo in the forest of Arden, Silvius and Orlando follow suit:

Silvius: If this be so, why blame you me to love you?

Orlando: If this be so, why blame you me to love you?

Silvius's repetition of the line extends the argument, for if Ganymede does not love any woman, and so will not proclaim his love for Phebe, who despite that rejection can love Ganymede anyway, then how can Phebe blame Silvius for proclaiming his love for her despite her rejection of him? Orlando simply repeats the line, which of course seems to make no sense at all in the context. Rosalind asks for clarification:

Rosalind: Who do you speak to, "Why blame you me to love you?"

Orlando: To her that is not here, nor doth not hear.

The pun is significant and Orlando's line is ironic. All of the characters, including Rosalind, assume the conjunction of here and hear—they will hear only if they are "here." Of course, the precise opposite is true. Phebe will not "hear" Silvius who is "here." Rosalind affirms her love for Orlando through her denials and while Orlando is "here" to hear he does not hear, and though Rosalind can "hear" Orlando, he thinks she is not "here." By this time the case of mistaken identity brought about by her pose has generated such confusion of speech that Rosalind is prompted to say: "Pray you, no more of this: 'tis like the howling of Irish wolves against the moon." At this point in the Forest of Arden, speech has become perilously perplexing: it does not accomplish recognition, and language becomes a howl, clarifying nothing. The quote of Stein's epigraph, then, moves from definition to confusion. Or to be more precise, it moves from an attempt to present love, to have it here and hear, to the howl for an unattainable object which can neither hear nor respond. Desire, which is illimitable, subverts its own quest for recognition through delimitable declarations and definitions.

The ironic awareness of the epigraph is echoed in the novel's allusion to and reliance upon the traditional literary significance of the sea. When the novel opens, Adele, Helen, and Mabel are on board ship enroute to Europe. Typically representative of a place where civilization's order and mores can be put into question, the novel's opening space not only refers back to the epilogue and Shakespeare's use of the pastoral Forest of Arden, but also relies upon the layers of connotation behind the use of the sea voyage in a tradition extending from the *Odyssey* into the eighteenth- and nineteenth-century novel. For Ulysses as well as Robinson Crusoe, the sea represented the seduction of illimitable possibility, the seduction of a dangerous adventure into the unknown. In *Q.E.D.* this will be a psychological journey. For during this voyage on the "wine colored sea"[14] Adele will not only be seduced into the passion of a socially unconventional love affair, but will also be seduced into the adventure of a psychological study of the two women with whom she is to become involved. These two companions, as the narrator points out, "would as the acquaintance progressed, undoubtedly expose large tracts of unexplored and unknown qualities, filled with new and strange excitements" (p. 53).

The energy of *Q.E.D.*'s echo of the literary sea voyage, however, is muted by irony. Adele describes herself as "not being of an heroic breed," (p. 74) and, a modern navigator, she affects a worldly weariness about embarking upon her journey: "Heigho its an awful grind," she remarks, "new countries, new people and new experiences all to see, to know and to understand" (p. 54). If Robinson Crusoe eagerly rebelled against his father's advocacy of the "middle life," Adele takes the father's part by posing genuine concern for the "middle class ideal" that would "avoid excitements and cultivate serenity" (p. 59). If Crusoe attempted to escape this sort of landlocked complacency by taking to the seemingly boundless possibilities of the sea, Adele describes the ocean as a "nice clean white inverted saucer," the "most confined space in the world" (p. 58). The sea has become domesticated. Even if Adele's two companions offer the adventure of new knowledge, the narrator, who seems but an echo of Adele's sensibility throughout the book, can cheerfully tame the connotations of the literary voyage's purpose by participating in Adele's worldly ironic stance: "A little knowledge is not a dangerous thing," the narrator tells us, "on the contrary it gives the most cheerful sense of completeness and content" (p. 53). While Adele's and the narrator's assertions are meant to cultivate a sense of serenity, the literary allusion to the sea cultivates a sense of excitement for the intrigue of the unknown. Adele, like Ulysses, will sail past the limit of legitimate exploration into a world in which neither etiquette nor convention can prescribe any safe rules of conduct. However, fearing what she most desires, Adele wards off with one hand what she beckons with the other. While Ulysses relied upon his infamous eloquence to help him navigate through a marvelous world of monsters, magicians, and usurpers, Adele anchors herself in her assertions. By that anchorage, no matter how far out to sea, she will protect herself from the challenges to her idealized moral commitments.

Through its allusions to the sea, the text can speak to a quest which is both desired and feared; allusions provide muted assertions, insights which are mere glimpses. This is precisely the status of Adele's allusion to Dante's *La Vita Nuova*. At the height of her tortured confusion over her growing involvement with Helen, Adele suddenly thinks she begins to understand the relationship. The nature of this new understanding is never articulated for the reader. It is referred to as an "insight" which instead of deepening, soon is in danger of becoming merely a "glimpse." However, upon reading *La Vita Nuova* in Tangiers, Adele finds the support she needs in that book, which suddenly becomes for her "divinely illuminated." She is able to "rejoice" in her "new understanding": "At last I begin to see what Dante is talking about and so there is something in my glimpse and it's alright and worthwhile" (p. 69).

La Vita Nuova is Dante's first work, the drama of his first meeting with Beatrice and the "Lord of Love." At the book's outset, the young poet announces that he will copy from his "book of memory" only those events significant to his growth as a lover and as a poet, the events significant to the period marking his "new life." As the poet struggles through the powerful, contradictory and often obscure effects of his growing love, he analyzes himself and the meaning of each event in his poems. At first this analysis is devoted to the young poet's self-pity, poetic pleas to Beatrice for mercy, and his sadness when his love for Beatrice is unreciprocated. His moment of illumination, the vision which gains him happiness, comes upon his realization that the material importance of his lady's "greeting" which was once "the end of all my desires"[15] is less important than the new, spiritual endeavor of exalting her through his poetry. To place the significance of his struggle in the new purpose of exalting Beatrice through his writing is, as the poet writes, to "place all my bliss in something that cannot fail me."[16] And finding a resting place in this first passionate struggle, he also finds future momentum. Beatrice will play a central role in his future works and it is to this insight that the last words of his book are devoted: " . . . if it be the wish of Him in whom all things flourish that my life continue for a few years, I hope to write of her that which has never been written of any other lady."[17]

If speech and writing are the object of desire in *La Vita Nuova*, language is implicated in what is incomprehensible, inarticulate, and mysterious. In the beginning of that work, the "Lord of Love" had visited the poet in a dream, uttering mysterious words whose significance the poet could not understand. Dante used the occasion for his first poem. That significance is not spelled out; rather Dante writes: "The true interpretation of the dream I described was not perceived by anyone then, but now it is very clear even to the least sophisticated."[18] *La Vita Nuova* is structured with this dual consciousness of time. With his final vision behind him when he sits down to copy from the "Book of Memory" at the beginning of the work, the drama's complexity yet unfolds gradually to lead the reader to the poet's final insight. By the end of the text, supposedly, we have accumulated the sense of the Lord of Love's words which are never directly spoken, interpreted or defined for us. The book, in essence, is a discussion of the effects of love on the poet's sensibility, and it is only by its effects that love is gradually comprehended. And the greatest effect, finally, for Dante is the motivation to write of that love. As it does for the young lover at the beginning of *La Vita Nuova*, love speaks in obscure ways for Adele at the point in *Q.E.D.* where Dante's text is introduced. It is impossible to name the insight Adele arrived at in reading that book in Tangiers; her silence as to the nature of her insight is an interesting echo of the silence of the Lord of Love. *Q.E.D.*, on the other hand, seems to stand as testimony to what Stein had absorbed from that book: the "divine illumination" to write about May, a decision that would idealize and retain a lost love, recuperate what otherwise could have been a wasted passion.

The possibility of wasted or betrayed passion is the subject of *The Wings of the Dove*, a book directly quoted in *Q.E.D.* Adele characterizes Helen, at one point, as Kate Croy:

What a condemned little prostitute it is, Adele said to herself between a laugh and a groan. I know there is no use asking for an explanation. Like Kate Croy she would tell me "I shall sacrifice nothing and nobody" and that's just her situation, she wants and will try for everything (p. 121).

Tipped off by this explicit reference to *The Wings of the Dove*, several critics have pointed out the similarities between James's style and Stein's.[19] The book's influence upon Stein was important in a more specific sense than this, however. The several congruities between the two books in terms of plot, characterization, and theme suggest that James's book helped Stein to formulate the presentation of her own relationship.

At the point in *The Wings of the Dove* where Kate says to Merton Densher: "I shan't sacrifice you; don't cry out till you're hurt. I shall sacrifice nobody and nothing, and that's just my situation, that I want and that I shall try for everything,"[20] her situation is strikingly similar to that of Helen's in *Q.E.D.* Both Kate and Helen have problematic family lives. Kate's father, a narrow-minded and unscrupulous fellow, has done "something wicked" in the past which has brought dishonor

upon the family. Similarly, Helen's father is a "brutal and at
the same time small-minded man who exercised great inge-
nuity in making himself unpleasant" (p. 73), and often refuses
his daughter enough money to live on. Both women are attracted to material and social success, but balk against making
concessions to their families' ambitions in that regard. "Of course
they are proud of her good looks, her cleverness and social
success," Mabel describes Helen to Adele, "but she won't get
married and she doesn't care to please the people her mother
wants her to belong to" (pp. 73-74). Kate's family, impoverished
by the circumstances of her father's dishonor, looks to the clever,
handsome Kate and her position of favor with her wealthy Aunt
Maud as redemption. Under Aunt Maud's guardianship, Kate
is being silently prodded into a relationship with Lord Mark.
Recognizing the limitations of her choice and freedom under
Aunt Maud, and having fallen in love with the impoverished
Morton Densher, whose position as a newspaper writer does
not meet with either her family's or Aunt Maud's approval,
Kate attempts to plot an escape from her Aunt. When her father
refuses to take her in, however, Kate's escape will ultimately
attempt to sacrifice neither her aunt, whose comfortable way
of life attracts her, nor her relationship with Merton. The economics of the situation, then, serve as a complication to the
love affairs in both books. Both Kate and Helen must take into
account, in their choice of love affairs, the expectations of a
third party whose financial backing is important to them. If
Kate Croy and Merton Densher must secretly plot around the
approval of Aunt Maud, Helen and Adele must plot in secret
around Mabel, whose subsidy of Helen for trips, gifts, and other
comforts seems to be her greatest attraction for Helen. Helen,
then, refuses to sacrifice either the comforts Mabel can offer,
or her relationship with Adele.

This makes Adele's situation very similar to Merton Densher's. If Stein explicitly characterized May as Kate Croy, she
may have been silently imaging herself in the position of the
young writer, Densher. Densher, essentially passive, "more a
respecter, in general, than a follower of custom,"[21] attracts Kate
because of his intelligence: "It was essentially on the side of
the mind that Densher was rich for her and mysterious and

strong; and he had rendered her in especial the sovereign service of making that element real."[22] Similarly, Adele characterizes herself as wanting things "only in order to understand them . . . all I want to do is to meditate endlessly and think and talk" (p. 80). She spends much of her time with Helen "announcing with great interest the result of her endless meditations" (p. 76). For Merton, Kate offers the attraction of being uniquely vital, for "it always seemed to him that she had more life than he to react from."[23] In this respect, both Merton and Adele are pupils. After Helen tells Adele that her inability to feel makes her face "almost annoyingly unlived and youthful," Adele responds with the conviction, "I could undertake to be an efficient pupil if it were possible to find an efficient teacher" (p. 60).

Her lessons in passion soon involve her in an uncomfortable secrecy and a policy of strategy vis-à-vis Mabel that is strikingly similar to Merton and Kate's subtle game with Aunt Maud. Kate assures Merton that these intricate maneuvers in the game with her aunt are a "pleasure" for there are "refinements—! . . . of consciousness, of sensation, of appreciation . . . things men don't know. They know in such matters almost nothing but what women show them."[24] Notably, both Kate and Helen show rather than tell, often forwarding their plots by means of portentous but ambiguous silences which both Merton and Adele must interpret and decide how to act upon. But it is important to point out that Kate's silence *per se* is not a subject of James's moralizing, since her silence arises from "neither ill will nor from duplicity, but from a failure of common terms—[Kate would never] reduce it to such a one's comprehension or put it within her convenience."[25] In the late James novel it is within this realm, intricately spun from the ambiguities of the unspoken, that the complex moral implications of the novel are worked out. In Stein's novel, on the other hand, Helen's silence finally becomes a subject for moralizing in and of itself. Helen moves from the characterization as an intriguing but "most silent being" at the beginning of the novel to someone who has formulated "a theory of the whole duty of silence" at the end. It is to the subject of Helen's "duty of silence" that Adele directs her speech at the end of the novel, a speech which, as we shall see, is both an impassioned plea to Helen and a denouncement of her.

The allusions—to Shakespeare, the sea, Dante, and James—in *Q.E.D.* speak to the way in which Stein formulated a literary identity for herself—the way in which she projected not only an image of herself in her affair, but an image of herself as writer and recorder of that affair. In a sense, these formulations, by means of allusions to other texts, were anchors, giving her a way to order and stabilize her perceptions in a sea of inchoate sensations. Previous literature could formulate these perceptions and then persuade her, as it could her character Adele when she reads Dante, that these insights were "alright and worthwhile." Yet, an identity is not to be formulated in this way without conflict and ambivalence, as her most powerfully suggestive allusion to *The Wings of the Dove* makes clear.

Alice B. Toklas was to mention *The Wings of the Dove* as the one book by James that Stein read several times, and Toklas was also to point out the "very direct connections" between Kate Croy and Helen.[26] Despite parallels to the James novel, not only in characterization, but also in theme and plot, Stein denied having read James in her early career at all. In the *Autobiography* she has her narrator Alice tell us that:

... [Gertrude] contends that Henry James was the first person in literature to find the way to the literary methods of the twentieth century. But oddly enough in all of her formative period she did not read him and was not interested in him. But as she often says one is always naturally antagonistic to one's parents and sympathetic to one's grandparents. The parents are too close, they hamper you, one must be alone. So perhaps that is the reason why only very lately Gertrude Stein reads Henry James.[27]

This would seem to be another case of "fortunate forgetting" on Stein's part; but as Harold Bloom, whose theory of the anxiety of influence Stein here seems not only to foresee but act out, comments:

Poetry, despite its publicists, is not a struggle against repression but is itself a kind of repression ... in response to other poems. ... Forgetting is anything but a liberating process. Every forgotten precursor becomes a giant in the imagination.[28]

Likening the relationship among the young poet, muse, and precursor to the "family romance" of Freud, Bloom delineates a struggle on the part of the young poet to attain a poetic identity and to "rescue" the muse from the precursor, a struggle which is fraught with all of the ambivalence of a love-hate relationship between parent and child. The young poet's quest for identity thus takes the form of a ritualized pattern, and the awareness of indebtedness creates a typically Freudian hostility:

The poet is condemned to learn his profoundest yearnings through an awareness of other selves. The poem is *within* him, yet he experiences the shame and splendor of *being found* by poems—great poems—*outside* him. To lose freedom in this center is never to forgive, and to learn the dread of threatened autonomy forever.[29]

The form which the "assertion against influence" takes, according to Bloom, is the young poet's deliberate misprision or misinterpretation of the parent poem; a misinterpretation which is meant to serve as a corrective.

Stein liked to use the word "precursor" to describe her relationship to Henry James, as Alice pointed out in her letters.[30] And as Stein herself pointed out in the quote from her *Autobiography* cited above, James was the "first person" to create the methods of the twentieth century, a project she was fond of claiming to have embarked upon more thoroughly herself. James's famous directive that a novel should render without a narrator's intrusion is but one of the obvious examples of the way in which James relied upon silence, the unspoken, to push traditional narrative form to its limit. As Shoshana Felman points out in her analysis of *The Turn of the Screw*, "narrative paradoxically becomes possible to the precise extent that a story becomes impossible—that a story precisely won't tell."[31] To tell—in forthright, outspoken terms—is to be "vulgar" in Jamesian terms, to attempt to eliminate "the indecision which inhabits meaning and . . . the ambiguity of the text."[32]

The similarities between Kate Croy and Helen suggest that

Stein had not only found a literary way of imaging May Bookstaver and her part in the relationship, but perhaps, more importantly, a way of interpreting and departing from her
precursor's text. Kate Croy is a character with whom we can
sympathize, despite—probably even because of—her ambiguous values. Stein reduces the ambiguity of the parent text. For
Helen's values, on the other hand, are made to stand in stark
opposition to Adele's; ultimately Helen is depicted as a "condemned prostitute." Helen's status as "prostitute" has interesting connotations in terms of Bloom's scheme, indicative
perhaps of the struggle the young Stein was engaged in. The
young poet, Bloom writes, is doomed to discover that "his word
is not his own word only, and his Muse has whored with many
before him."[33]

To the extent that Adele represents Stein in the text, then,
Stein's project in *Q.E.D.* became one of concretizing, of bringing
to a halt the ambiguities of a parent text by means of moral
scrutiny. Adele, however, as we have seen, is herself a projection, a displacement and therefore a metonomy of and for Stein.
The several allusions to other texts in *Q.E.D.* speak to an ironic
awareness of the ways in which language, because of the insistence of desire, is implicated in deceit, confusion, and the
incomprehensible contained within and represented by silence.
This ironic awareness makes Adele's outspoken position tenuous. A novel which attempts to clarify, *Q.E.D.* indicates its
fascination with the ambiguity of silence.

III. The Story

After Nietzsche (and, indeed, after any "text"), we can no longer
hope ever "to know" in peace. (Paul de Man)

By means of its allusions, *Q.E.D.* seems to speak through
silent textual constructions. These silent constructions often
counterbalance the explicit constructions of the novel, revealing an important tension. If, through its allusion to the literary
sea voyage the text can articulate a quest for knowledge, that
quest is complicated by being both feared and desired. The
epigraph, typically a device to announce the thematic inten-

tions of the text, complicates the issue further. For in that quote, the attempt to articulate desire moves from definition through confusion to a final explosive release in a howl: language finally seems inadequate. Despite the ironic laughter behind her selection of this particular quote from Shakespeare's comedy, a laughter which seems aimed at her own project to describe, define, and delineate a passionate affair, Stein relies upon metaphors of definite expression and clear vision to develop her subject and theme.

In this novel definite expression is formulated and predicated upon logic. The novel's title is but one indication of Stein's attempt to render with mathematical precision. Several critics have pointed to the importance of the metaphor of geometry to the book's structure. Michael Hoffman, for example, has demonstrated the ways in which the book shows a careful structural balance around the theme of a triangle:

> There are three books within the novelette, each bearing the name of one of the sides of the triangle. There are three trips to Europe. There is a balance among the three personalities present within the triangle. The slow-moving and sensual Adele is played off against the prudish and calculating (Mabel). Both are striving to cement the affection of the passionate and headstrong Helen (the hypotenuse if you will). Three years is the length of time that elapses in the story, with the second year the high point of the relationship between Adele and Helen.[34]

All of the characters, major and minor, are neatly typified and categorized in the beginning of the novel. This delineation into types and categories not only defines but limits the characters. Adele's fellow passengers on the ship are "of some abjectly familiar type that one knew so well that there would be no real need of recognizing their existence" (p. 53). The two women whose existence must be recognized, Mabel and Helen, are fit into types according to their European heritage. Their American nature seems to introduce an element of corruption into what these types could have been in their "ideal completeness." Helen is the "American version of the English handsome girl" who

in her ideal completeness ... would have been unaggressively determined, a trifle brutal and entirely impersonal; a woman of passions
but not of emotions, capable of long sustained action, incapable of
regrets. In this American edition it amounted at its best to no more
than a brave bluff (pp. 54-55).

Mabel, the New England spinster type, has

a face that in its ideal completeness would have belonged to the decadent days of Italian greatness. It would never now express completely a nature that could hate subtly and poison deftly. In the
American woman the aristocracy had become vulgarized and the power
weakened (pp. 54-55).

The categorization of these characters seems hopefully to hold
out an explanation for the frustrations of the affair before the
story of that affair even begins. These two young American
women imitate the corruptions of the European aristocracy but,
because they are simply imitative, they lack the force of the
sophistication and subtlety of the original. Their power and
morality is thus both weakened and limited. Stein's explanation obviously relies upon a familiar Jamesian theme—the corruption and moral decadence of European aristocracy and the
effect of this class upon the young American heroine who comes
into contact with it. Like James, Stein introduces a moral, vital,
and "original" young heroine who is meant to withstand and
counter the corruptions of European influence. Stein attempts
to accomplish this departure from European influence with her
character Adele.

Adele is the only character to escape the limitations of a
category. She has no counterpart in a European type and, thoroughly American, acts "with the freedom of movement and the
simple instinct for comfort that suggest a land of laziness and
sunshine" (p. 55). America and its sunshine, in this text, suggest a brand of sensuality which is meant to counterpoint the
"darker," more obscure realm of desire which Helen and Mabel
occupy. Sunshine suggests a clean simplicity and pure morality, that which is "natural"; a realm most often associated with
Adele, it is the outward projection of her capacity for insight
and for her ability to "see clearly."

In this respect, the realm of sunshine which Adele occupies is part of an important symbolic network of light and vision which, with its adjunct in logic and definite expression, structures the novel. Each of the three books opens with a landscape or environment described in terms of its lighting and moves to a statement about Adele's growth in insight into the affair.

Book I, devoted to Adele, opens with the three characters sitting in the brilliant sunshine on the deck of the ship. While Helen and Mabel indulge in the hypocrisies of social convention, Adele plays in the sunshine; when their obscure game becomes too complicated and confusing, she seeks relief by basking in the hot white sunshine of Tangiers, where the glimpse of insight into the affair she received on board ship becomes "divinely illuminated" upon reading Dante.

Book II is devoted to her rival, Mabel, and moves inside, significantly opening with a description of the way in which Mabel, who has a "talent for atmosphere" (p. 70) has arranged her room so that the firelight focuses and centers attention on itself. If Adele is associated with the force and power of nature, sunlight, which also, by the text's logic, somehow endows her with a fuller consciousness, Mabel is associated with the more civilized but weaker form of light, firelight, and this realm seems artfully controlled by Mabel to foster only a semi-conscious awareness on the part of her guests. The firelight leaves "the decorations in obscurity or rather inspires a faith in their being good," and she had "arranged her room so that one enjoyed one's companions and observed consciously only the pleasant fireplace" (p. 70). In Book II, despite her persistent attempt to consciously understand the affair, Adele becomes increasingly implicated and involved in Mabel's realm, which she does not understand. At the end of Book II, Adele is once again basking in the sunshine, this time "lying on the green earth of the sunny English hillside communing with herself" (p. 95) about the affair, but this time only tenuously certain that she does "have occasional sparkling glimpses of faith" (p. 97). Glimpses of insight have turned into glimpses of faith, a measure of Adele's growing participation in what is irrationally felt rather than rationally perceived.

Yet, Book III insistently repeats the pattern of the other two books and the opening description of Book III blatantly attempts to recuperate the values associated with the previous symbolism of sunshine and America. The book opens with a comparison of London where "the dreary sun, moon, and stars . . . look like painted imitations on the ceiling of a smoke-filled room" (p. 100) and America, where the clean, white winter landscape is "without mystery and without complexity" (p. 101). Adele rejoices in "clear-eyed Americanism" and the "passionless intelligence" of American faces; and the narrative description seems to be a forceful reaction to and rejection of Adele's growing implication in Mabel's realm of artifice: "perhaps the weight of stains necessary to the deepest understanding might be washed away . . ." (p. 101).

Adele's story may well have been entitled "crime and transcendence." Caught by her desire for Helen in a game that seems immoral and dishonest to her, Adele yet insists upon escaping into a realm where she can judge the very game she has become implicated in. This is a realm in which, as Adele proclaims at the end of the novel, things are seen clearly, "as they are" and not as one "would make them." Adele's "transcendence" is aided and abetted by her Americanism, her association with sunshine and the great outdoors, her ability to "see"—all qualities which are meant to guarantee her a privileged outside position. The repetitive pattern of the three books seems a desperate attempt to recuperate and maintain this position of moral innocence. If Adele manages to arrive at some insight into the affair at the end of each "book," this insight only becomes muddled and confused again in the face of her desire. That the last book ends on Adele's final insight into the affair is no guarantee that the insight is actually final, since we are entitled by the repetitive pattern of the novel to imagine the whole cycle beginning again. "Seeing clearly" in the last analysis does not seem to provide sufficient explanation.

Ultimately, the attempt to find an explanation constitutes the drama of *Q.E.D.* Adele's attempts to maintain her moral integrity are less intense than her attempts to maintain an integrated notion of herself by the concentrated scrutiny and analysis of each event and nuance of the drama of the unfolding relationship. As her moral principles become more tenuous in the face of her desire, Adele becomes more adamantly concerned with the struggle to interpret, articulate and explain to herself the course desire is charting for her.

In this respect, Adele is projected as the antithesis of Helen who is a "most silent being" and who remains aloof to Adele's project of "criticiz[ing] and examin[ing] herself and her ideas with tireless interest" (p. 76). Helen keeps her motivation and feelings in silence, a mystery that intrigues and irritates Adele. Helen's behavior seems to Adele to offer a multitude of "possibilities." Is Helen genuinely fond of her, playing a game with her, testing her, or simply trying to teach her a lesson? Adele must test each possibility by articulating it to herself or to Helen. Helen's response to Adele is either silent, or evasive— as when she tells Adele that she cares for her "more than you know and less than you think" (p. 65), or tearfully resistant, as when she accuses Adele of being too "ruthless" in her analysis: "You trample everything ruthlessly under your feet without considering whether or not you kill something precious and without being changed or influenced by what you so brutally destroy" (p. 88). While Adele tries to find a plateau of stability and certainty by continuously attempting to find "the key," Helen's responses serve to keep possibilities open. "She gives me no means of taking hold," Adele says to herself, "and the key of the lock is surely not in me" (p. 63). In typical fashion, Adele doubts even this possibility and subjects her own motivation to scrutiny. "As for me is it another little indulgence of my superficial emotions or is there any possibility of my really learning to realise stronger feelings. . . . Certainly it is very difficult to tell" (p. 64). Adele's attempts to "tell" often end in silence and a stalemate with herself or in discussion with others.

Ironically, then, the text supports Helen's point of view. Adele's persistent attempts at analysis do seem, if not "ruthless," most often superfluous. Her arguments do not persuade Helen, and often not even herself, and they do not change the course of the relationship. If Helen's silence often prompts Adele's attempts to explain it, Adele's most important insights, the insight she reaches in Tangiers, for example, are never articulated for the reader but are kept wrapped in silence. Indeed, silence becomes a powerful force in the text and begins

to take on an amorphous character and changeable personality
of its own, at times representing feelings which are incomprehensible, moods that "roar and menace" (p. 86), thoughts that
can not be formulated, plateaus of intimacy, and finally a weapon
that irritates and frustrates Adele's attempts at a final understanding. In Book I, especially, the text's silences not only preserve what cannot be told, but often seem to propel the course
of the relationship and the narrative. Even the typography of
the text suggests this—two or three paragraphs form blocks of
narrative, blocks separated from each other by a blank white
space. At the end of each of these narrative blocks, Adele has
usually been brought to the point of mystification. As though
there could be no immediately suitable transition or explanation for her feelings, the blank space allows for the brief
appreciation of this mystification before there is a new attempt
to launch into narration.

If Adele values expression, and Helen values silence, at least
both women seem earnest and sincere in their advocacy of these
values. Helen tells Adele that "somehow I don't feel that your
words really express you" and is sincerely impatient with Adele's
attempts to articulate and analyze the relationship. If Helen's
patience with ambiguity intrigues Adele by representing "so
many possibilities" Adele is quick to add that "then there is
Mabel." Mabel is the other "gentleman" of the relationship;
both she and Adele are represented as identifying with male
poses, and the triangular lesbian affair often seems to be the
struggle of two men vying for the affections of the more feminine Helen. Adele identifies with a male pose that is intellectually analytic—"I once thought I knew something about
women" (p. 62), she sighs at one point—and impatient with
social amenities—"I always did thank God I wasn't born a
woman" (p. 58), she exclaims after Mabel and Helen have in-
dulged in a particularly elaborate and annoying exchange of
social niceties. Mabel is the young gallant who sways Helen
by gifts and other economic enticements ("alas for an unbut-
tered influence say I," moans Adele at one point), and "has the
unobtrusive good manners of a gentleman" which take the form
of a more sophisticated understanding of unspoken social relations. Of the two characteristics, the latter poses the stronger

threat to Adele. Mabel uses language in ways that Adele, who strives for clear thinking and honest expression, does not understand and condemns. Mabel is able to conceal her feelings behind language fraught with the "double meanings" with which Adele is so impatient, and which are represented in the book as a form of moral hypocrisy. Mabel is represented as using this method of concealment as a weapon to manipulate others and to gain control of the relationship. In this way, she becomes a sort of master of ceremonies who begins to implicate Helen and Adele into her game on her own terms. Mabel listens to the discussions between Helen and Adele "as if it were a play and enacted for her benefit and queerly enough although the disputants were much in earnest in their talk and in their oppositions, it was a play and enacted for her benefit" (pp. 60-61). If Mabel is a master of ceremonies, she is also a master of pose. In this respect, in Book II, a book devoted to Mabel, the relationship shifts into a new key and a different phase.

There are two major discussions between Mabel and Adele in Book II, discussions in which Adele attempts to discover Mabel's part in the affair and the nature of her influence over Helen. Adele tries to characterize her tactic in these discussions as direct confrontation: she meets Mabel with "frank bravado" (p. 73) and "hot directness" (p. 86). Actually, the important point of her curiosity—her growing attachment to and desire for Helen—remains unspoken, and since it is unspoken Mabel strategically uses it to her advantage. Mabel colors the presentation of her narrative about Helen's family life so that she gives the implication of possessing Helen's past, and therefore Helen. Because this implication, and so much of real importance to Adele, is unspoken, Adele can only resent Mabel in silence.

However, Mabel not only plays upon her knowledge of Helen's past, but upon her own past relationship with Adele as well. Adele is one of her "selected few" (p. 72) and Mabel proceeds to exploit Adele's feelings of obligation toward their previous friendship. Based upon what Mabel supposes for her own purpose to be Adele's previous loyalty to her, she proceeds to maneuver Adele into an awkward position by asking her for advice about Helen. Adele can only resort to an ironic retort, which she feels is "quite satisfactorily vulgar" (p. 84). Mabel, on her part, chooses to misinterpret Adele's irony. She accepts Adele's advice "literally," and by doing so once again gains control of the situation and of Adele: "it is such a comfort that you understand everything," she tells Adele, "and one can speak to you openly about it all" (p. 85). Mabel continues to use this professed intimacy with Adele as a platform from which to speak. After giving Adele a more detailed account of her past relationship with Helen, an account which badly upsets Adele, Mabel claims that "nothing but her great regard for Adele would have made it possible for her to speak as she had done" (p. 93). Adele understands Mabel's ploy and decides that she owes nothing to Mabel, but while Mabel continues to spin this fictional intimacy with Adele in order to maintain and forward her own relationship with Helen, Adele continues helpless in the face of her desire and her unwillingness to express it directly to Mabel.

Mabel, however, has, as we remember, a talent for creating "atmosphere" and the atmosphere of her influence pervades Book II. This is the atmosphere of artifice—of the posing and deceit involved in a competitive game of desire. It is a game which soon begins to implicate Helen and Adele. While Mabel keeps up her cheerful but false pose of intimacy with Adele, Helen and Adele begin to allow "conventions of secrecy" and "conventions of silence" to govern their relationship. These conventions only apply to the game between the two of them: "To Adele's consciousness the necessity of this secrecy was only apparent when they were together. She felt no obligation to conceal this relation from their friends" (p. 75). Adele is caught between trying to foist the responsibility of this pose onto Helen, who she claims would shut her mind to any explicit statement of probabilities, and admitting that she, too, is responsible for "not bringing things to a head" because she is unsure "of the fidelity of her own feelings" (pp. 94-95). Both women find it convenient not to make any explicit statements about the nature of their relationship, for both women essentially want to remain passive in terms of taking responsibility for the future of the relationship. Adele claims that she has not the "inclination nor the power to take Mabel's place" and that it is "Helen's affair" (p. 94), and Helen, on her part, asks Adele: "have I done anything but be passive while you did as you pleased? I have been willing to endure it all, but I have not taken one step to hold you" (p. 107).

Ultimately, Adele is unwilling to take Mabel's place because she is unwilling to take any position at all. Scrupulous honesty will not allow her to take the "false position" of admitting more than she feels for Helen, as Mabel plays on the pose of feeling more than she does for Adele; and yet by not taking a position, Adele, in her quest for explanations, is unable to find a suitable interpretation for the affair. She is never sure that she has interpreted Helen's feelings correctly, and when she tries to define Helen she sees two Helens at odds with each other—one with a nature of brutal coarseness and a point of view that is aggressively unsympathetic, and another who "possesses a purity and intensity of feeling" and has an "infinitely tender patience" (p. 81). Adele is never sure which interpretation it is to her advantage to believe in; but the advantage of maintaining silence with Helen about the conditions of their relationship is the advantage of being able to indulge in the intrigue of meditating endlessly about Helen's ambiguities.

This is ineffective in the competition with Mabel, however. If Mabel can derive the power of speech from the innuendo of false poses, Adele does not have a suitable weapon in her arsenal with which to retaliate. Deciding that she is "willing to fight in any way that Mabel likes," she writes a letter which is intended to make matters "clear to her" and yet to "complicate it in a fashion that she loves." The attempt is ineffectual, for Mabel has a great appreciation for the literal when it suits her, and Adele's letter literally "says nothing":

"My dear Mabel" she wrote, "either you are duller than I would like to think you or you give me credit for more good-natured stupidity than I possess. If the first supposition is correct then you have nothing to say and I need say nothing; if the second then nothing that you would say would carry weight so it is equally unnecessary for you to say anything. If you don't understand what I am talking about then I am talking about nothing and it makes no difference, if you do then there's enough said" (p. 93).

The letter's ominous obfuscation barely represents its intended challenge to Mabel, who chooses to ignore it entirely. Instead of challenging Mabel about the fictitious intimacy she is creating about her relationship with Adele, the letter is a plea for silence, both Mabel's and Adele's. Adele's battle with Mabel's authority over the relationship is a battle against having the relationship authored at all.

If Mabel has control of a drama that directs the course of the relationship, the narrator compensates Adele for her inability to silence Mabel. Book II is entitled "Mabel," but very little of it is devoted to her as a character. In typical fashion, the narrator at the beginning of the book typecasts her in a way which seeks to limit her power and influence. Mabel is deemed to be a "failure as an individual. Her passions in spite of their intensity failed to take effective hold on the objects of her desire. ... She lacked the vital force necessary to win" (p. 71). Consistently characterized as deceitful and hypocritical, Mabel is hardly a "rounded" character. Significantly, her most important revelation about the nature of her relationship with Helen is kept in silence; we get only Adele's reaction of overwhelming repulsion and disgust. In this respect, the narrator borrows some of Mabel's strategies. The narrator not only effectively uses the unspoken to her advantage, but she also manipulates her presentation of Mabel and of the past events of the affair in order to ultimately control and possess Helen, and to gain the reader's sympathies for this action. If Mabel has some sort of influence over Helen, she is allowed to have very little positive influence over the reader's sympathies.

The narrator thus protects Adele from what Adele perceives to be the distasteful task of "authoring" the relationship. To do so might implicate her in the deceitful maneuvers and poses of a competitive game of desire. But the "condition of silence" which Helen and Adele maintain is also a refusal to stabilize the ambiguous conditions of their relationship by taking a definite position. The force of their desire made both of them unwilling "ever to venture on an ultimatum for they realized that they would not be constant to it" (p. 107). In Book III they share a brief interlude of "silent intimacy." However, Adele is ultimately more eager for explanations than for ambiguities and in order to arrive at an explanation, one of them must decide upon a definite position.

Adele would clearly like Helen to make the decision. Despite the many self-doubting questions Adele asks herself about her part in the relationship, when Adele's desire for stabilizing the relationship is the strongest, she finds the greatest need to thrust the responsibility for the affair upon Helen. It is "Helen's affair" and Helen must choose between Mabel and Adele, while Adele waits in the wings. In Book III, Helen begins to win this position away from Adele and in a "triumph of passivity" (p. 112) she paradoxically manipulates Adele into "submission" by forcing the "burden of choice" and initiative upon Adele. Helen escapes making a choice, and Adele feels herself put into the position of maintaining the relationship, a burden which, since she begins with the premise that it is not her affair to begin with, would understandably involve her in what she feels to be a series of "false positions."

Though she increasingly resents the lack of "openness" that results, Adele at the same time uses the "false position" to maintain the relationship. When Adele discovers, for instance, that she and Helen have "pulses" which are "differently timed" she forces herself to go "further than she could in honesty because she was unable to refuse anything to one who had given all. It was a false position" (p. 104). The rhetoric of honesty vies with the rhetoric of boundless desire. To be honest would be to risk losing Helen. Unwilling to risk that, Adele counters Helen's "triumph of passivity" by maintaining false positions in order to maintain the relationship until Helen should make her choice.

This double bind becomes a triple bind when the three women meet in Italy. All of the women maintain the "false position" of pretending that there are no problems among them. For a brief moment, Adele dominates the scene and is in control of the situation. She is happy with this new feeling of control because she feels that "she had shown herself strong enough to realise power and yet be generous" (p. 124). This impulse of generosity can only be temporarily maintained, however, for in reality Adele is trying to satisfy three contradictory demands: keeping Helen happy, keeping Mabel happy by pretending that she doesn't care for Helen, and keeping herself happy by trying to be honest. Adele gets weary of trying to "keep it all going"; but she again thrusts the responsibility for this defection off onto Helen. Helen, she notes, "seems less successfully than ever to support the strain" (p. 125) and Mabel once again gains control of the relationship.

Adele has always been less interested in winning Helen than in understanding her: "I want things too," Adele explains to Helen, "but only in order to understand them and I never go and get them" (p. 80). However, the struggle of maintaining the relationship in order to understand Helen has been trying to Adele all along; she alternates between her longing for peace and her longing for Helen, a longing which inevitably disturbs her "happy serenity." In Book III, Adele is eager to concede the game and Helen entirely to Mabel. "If you think it will be better if I clear out I will go," she carefully explains to Helen. "I owe you so much for all that you have taught me" (p. 120). She keeps close watch for signs of "the end of the story" and in her desire for a "definite ending" she begins to lose momentum in her struggle with Mabel. Reverting to feeling guilty that "she is stealing the property of another" (p. 110) her rationalization becomes a concession to Mabel: Mabel will win eventually anyway because of her gifts to Helen. Adele can not convince herself to sustain the battle with Mabel; and to keep the possibilities of the relationship open is too painful: "All her actual consciousness found the definite ending of the situation a great relief. As long as one is firmly grasping the nettles there is no sting. The bitter pain begins when the hold begins to relax" (p. 113).

The appeal of a definite ending and the certainty it would provide prompt Adele to forget her own complicity in the "conditions" of the relationship and to define Helen's values as completely different from her own. Proud of her own generous impulse to try to satisfy the boundless desire of everyone involved, Adele yet impatiently accuses Helen of wanting to sacrifice nothing and nobody. Unwilling to confront Mabel herself, she accuses Helen of being "a condemned prostitute" for toadying to Mabel. The "condition of silence" sours into a "condition of deliberate deceit"—on Helen's part, worthy of a lecture from

Adele: "You hide yourself behind your silences. . . . Nothing is too good or holy for clear thinking and definite expression" (p. 132). Though she accuses Helen of "hating conclusions," Adele continues unwilling to conclude things herself. Still proclaiming her love for Helen, still impatient with her, and still unable to "find the key of the lock" of interpreting her, Adele's last decision is that the affair has "come very near being a deadlock" (p. 133). And so the book concludes by coming "very near" to conclusion.

Stein appended "finis" to a text which displayed and was caught up in a ceaselessly repetitive cycle of desire—a round of yearning to keep possibilities open succeeded by a yearning to foreclose them. Closure becomes the last in a series of the novel's "false positions"—false though they maintain the very desire that generates them. And so Mabel maintains a false position in order to maintain her relationship with Helen, and so Adele maintains her "false position" in order to ultimately get an explanation from Helen, and so the novel maintains the "false" schema of beginning, middle, and end to help Adele explain herself, and so, as Stein hopes, the choice of the epigraph from Shakespeare will point out that it may have all been a case of mistaken identity from the start.

But if "positions" are only "false," the relationship is in danger of not being authored at all. Adele decides to struggle with Mabel on Mabel's terms, and if her attempts to silence Mabel end in her own silence, the narrator vies with Mabel more effectively. And so the novel's struggle becomes one of diminishing the false lover's echo to silence. And so Stein vies with James for a way of portraying Helen, and so Alice vies with May for Gertrude, and so I vie with Adele for the "real Adele" and the critics for the "real Stein." And so Stein was to contend with her own version of *Q.E.D.* Laying her "outspoken" text to rest in the Florentine chest in her study, her next three novels are the preoccupied and continuous reinterpretation of a triangular affair.

II

Fernhurst: Place and Propriety

Without invading any law of social propriety or doing violence to one of the sacred instincts of her nature, [the college girl] will find a thousand womanly ways to serve. (President of Vassar, 1873, justification for a woman's education)[1]

I. "Too Outspoken"

It is probable that Gertrude Stein did not attempt to publish her second completed novel, *Fernhurst*, because she considered it to be, like *Q.E.D.*, "too outspoken." As Leon Katz has shown, Stein's model for her second novel was an event that involved people well known to Stein and others. For years, Gertrude, her brother Leo, and their circle of friends had been following the development of a scandalous affair at Bryn Mawr. The college president, Martha Carey Thomas, had been living with an English professor and good friend, Mary Gwinn. In the mid-nineties, Thomas hired Alfred Hodder, an old friend of Gertrude and Leo's from Harvard, to teach at Bryn Mawr. Hodder had been a brilliant student of William James. He was, however, more romantically than academically inclined. After arriving at Bryn Mawr with his common-law wife and children, he became involved with Mary Gwinn. Thomas was furiously jealous, but there was little she could do to stop the relationship.

In 1904, after years of serving as a most intriguing subject of gossip for all those even remotely associated with Bryn Mawr or Harvard, Gwinn and Hodder ran away to Europe where they were married.[2] Stein's portrait of Martha Carey Thomas would have been easily recognized; moreover, Stein introduced her narrative with a strong polemic against women's colleges. Stein, then, never sought the publication of this doubly outspoken manuscript as a self-contained novel. Instead, she incorporated the narrative, with only minor revisions, and without her introductory polemics, into the later project of writing *The Making of Americans*, effectively obscuring, if not burying entirely references to people and events.

Consequently, it has only been with the recent publication of Gertrude Stein's early writings that *Fernhurst* has come to light as Stein's second completed novel. The novel has not excited a great deal of critical commentary; but what commentary there is simply labels the novel as "crude," "jagged," "lacking focus," or "unsuccessful."[3] Having dismissed the text as a serious literary enterprise, critics find a redeeming value in it as a sort of biographical supplement, as a way of providing a personal portrait of Stein in 1904, when she wrote the novel. Kay Armatage, for example, assessing Stein's position as a feminist, relies upon a straightforward summary of the first five pages of *Fernhurst* for her assessment, for the narrator's statement seems to indicate quite clearly Stein's connections to the nineteenth-century women's movement.[4] Katz, Bridgman, and Mellow, on the other hand, have focused upon the narrative to the exclusion of the narrator's initial polemics in an attempt to position Stein by pointing out her identification with one character or another.[5] While all of these critics achieve their placement of Stein by focusing upon one section of the novel to the exclusion of the other, the narrative, as we shall see, does not only, or simply, demonstrate the premises of the opening polemic. And too, Stein's conflicting senses of self generate a number of possible identifications, yet she too insists, especially in her polemic, upon a definite position. The critical impulse to locate Stein, I would claim, participates in the narrator's own desire in *Fernhurst* to achieve a coherent, integrated positioning, an identity. The vehemence with which Stein insists upon a definite position indicates the depths of the potentially subversive crisis being repressed.

Since the articulation of a coherent, integrated position is usually the goal of any argumentative strategy, it is significant that *Fernhurst* begins in a highly rhetorical argumentative mode. In the opening pages, Stein's narrator considers the value of a college education for women, a subject that Stein had previously addressed in a speech delivered in 1898 when she had been a medical student. On one level, Stein's polemic at the beginning of *Fernhurst* is an argument with an earlier sense of self. There are indications throughout *Fernhurst* that a more savvy Stein is attempting to come to terms, realistically, with a formerly more naive self. For that reason, it would be useful to look at the opinion she advocated in her speech of 1898, an opinion she was to exactly reverse six years later in *Fernhurst*.

Although by 1898 a college education for women was becoming an increasingly acceptable idea, at least in the northeast and midwest, it was still enough of a subject of debate to provoke a number of rhetorical defenses. Stein mentioned, for example, at the beginning of her speech, entitled "The Value of a College Education for Women," that people in the northeast had a very different and a more liberal idea about education and she indicated that she saw herself defending this idea to a more conservative southern group of women.[6] As Sheila Rothman has pointed out, the terms of these rhetorical defenses were guided by an image of what proper womanhood was. Having proven that women could meet the rigors of education without going insane, it became important for those defending women's education at the turn of the century to argue that women would not become ignobly competitive or ambitious, but instead would remain devoted, in a wiser and more prepared way, for the duties of their special sphere.[7] The image defended, then, was one of the noble woman who would "tame," purify, and nurture society, the educated mother and intelligently supportive wife.

In advocating the importance of education for women in her speech of 1898, Stein not only assumed the truth of this image of women and the efficacy of arguing for it, but also reinforced

it by alluding to and extending the argument of Charlotte Perkins Gilman's book, *Women and Economics*. Because Stein relied very heavily upon the logic of this book to explain her own
position and situation, it is important to discuss its argument.
Gilman was an optimistic social Darwinist who had argued
that traditional marital arrangements had turned women into
over-sexed economic dependents. Because marriage and child-
bearing were the only approved activities open to them, women
were forced into cultivating an extreme form of femininity not
only as a way of attracting a mate but also as the only way of
earning a livelihood. Women were thus trapped by the tendency
to carry "sex distinctions to an excessive degree"; and, because
"the more widely the sexes are differentiated the more forcibly
are they attracted to each other," traditional sexual roles inevitably resulted in morbid sexuality to the great detriment of
the progress of the human race.[8]
Gilman stressed instead the "human traits" that men and
women share. She did not discourage marriage or maternity,
but argued instead for a new way of perceiving and defining
traditional roles. The emancipated mother, she argued, is a
much better mother who will contribute more effectively to the
progress of the human race.
Although Gilman may have mildly shocked her readers by
equating traditional marital arrangements with prostitution,
it is easy to understand why she was still a remarkably popular
writer, for she appealed to, rather than threatened, the assumptions of a progressively minded Victorian audience. She
optimistically subverted the threat of Darwinism by assuming
that the human race is capable of evolving toward perfection,
maintained the supreme importance of motherhood, to which
she devoted an entire chapter, and most forcefully, perhaps,
identified social evil with excessive sexuality, thus appealing
to Victorian prudery.
It is clear that Stein swallowed these assumptions for the
sake of Gilman's emphasis on a woman's "human" traits rather
than her sexual identity. In her speech of 1898, Stein followed
Gilman's lead in arguing against women's traditional status
as "commodities to be sold into marriage," emphasized the importance of the new image of the "well-rounded" mother de-

voted to husband, career, and children, and argued against the
dangers of excessive sexuality to which women were apparently
especially prone due to their traditionally defined gender roles.
In the natural order of things, Stein argued, citing examples
from the animal kingdom, the woman "only becomes a female
during her motherhood. She is not concerned with sex at any
other time." Paraphrasing Gilman, Stein insisted that traditional marital arrangements have created "an overdeveloped
sex desire that has turned a creature that should have been
first a human being and then a woman into one that is a woman
first and always and a human being only if it so happens."
Gilman's outlook had been optimistic; so was Stein's solution.
A college education, she contended, would "rightly realign and
purify" the sexual drives and prepare a woman to live a self-
reliant life.[9]

Six years later Stein had to account for what would seem to
be two rather paradoxical situations if viewed in terms of the
logic and the solution of this speech: her own, and the Bryn
Mawr affair upon which she was to base her *Fernhurst* narrative. Both Martha Carey Thomas and Mary Gwinn had been
fervent feminists, committed to educating women for their own
careers and seemingly firmly committed to their own. And yet,
Mary Gwinn "who had hitherto arrogantly eschewed all acquaintance with men" had "succumbed wholly to Hodder's fascination" and had been persuaded to leave Thomas, career, and
causes, for marriage to him.[10] On the other hand, in the terms
of her own kind of logic, Stein's own situation was no less
paradoxical. Medical school had hardly succeeded in "purifying
her sexual drive." In the last year of her studies she had met
May Bookstaver, and the emotional trials of that love affair
had probably contributed to the "boredom" she had proclaimed
as the reason for her lack of interest in her courses. The difficulty is expressed in a more generalized form by a disillusioned question posed by her narrator at the outset of *Fernhurst*:
"What! does a reform start hopeful and glorious with a people
to remake and all sex to destroy only to end in the same old
homes with the same men and women in their very same
place."[11] To account for this sad outcome, the narrator of *Fernhurst* once again considers the value of a college education for

women. Stein's new attitude toward this topic is complete skepticism. Her narrator, who is the vehicle of this attitude, poses as the disillusioned idealist, who, as Adele had in *Q.E.D.*, insists that we see things as they are. *Fernhurst*, like *Q.E.D.*, tries hard to be a realistic novel.

Significantly, within the first paragraph of *Fernhurst*, narrative strategies are immediately replaced by polemical strategies. In the first paragraph the narrator attempts to tell a story. She introduces a setting—a small women's college—and a character—an anonymous guest of honor who is addressing an audience at the college. However, the action of the narrative, the guest of honor's speech, is halted at the moment it begins. And the action is halted because the narrator distrusts the strategies of the guest of honor. These strategies consist of baiting her audience with praise "clothed" in the "technical language of the hearer's profession" (p. 3). This is "dangerous" according to the narrator, for it simply succeeds in flattering the audience's illusions. This particular speaker flatters her audience by telling them that "we college women we are always college girls" (p. 3). After delivering her line, which will be the topic of the narrator's own little speech, the speaker and her mode of doublespeak and ambiguous praise are summarily dismissed by the narrator. We can surmise she is impatient both with narration and her character for the same reason. Both utilize forms of flattery and illusion; what is needed is more straightforward language. The narrator thus mounts the podium herself in order to make sure that we understand that appearances are not reality, and that there is a "subtle mockery" beneath the guest of honor's apparent praise.

The woman who takes pride in remaining a "college girl" all of her life, according to the narrator, is a woman who has deluded herself into believing that the "superficial latin and cricket" which she learns at college have any real effectiveness in the "male" world of action and power. The colleges women attend are simply "ancient finishing schools" in disguise, and the courses they take in "classics and liberty" are simply the replacements for "the accomplishments of a lady" (p. 4).

This is what is at issue in the speech, in fact: women's effectiveness in "the affairs of the big world" and the ways in which their power in this realm is still limited. Because education has simply given them "acquired culture" rather than "vital capacity," women still derive their power surreptitiously, by insisting upon the privileges of a traditional and protected status: "I saw the other day a college woman resent being jostled by her male competitors in a rush for position—in spite of all training she was an American woman still, entitled to rights and privileges and no more willing to adopt male standards in a struggle than her grandmother" (p. 4). The woman who epitomizes the ploy of using underhanded and immoral means to attain and maintain power is Miss Thornton, who is the dean of the college of *Fernhurst*. Much abuse is heaped upon Miss Thornton for "the contradiction in her doctrine and the danger of her method" (p. 7). This contradiction consists of setting up an institution where "in accordance with the male idea" the college would be governed by the students themselves. In truth, however, all power is centered in the dean, who exercises this power and maintains it "by an admirable system of espionage and influence" interrupted by "occasional bald exercises of authority and not infrequent ignominious retreats" (pp. 5-6).

The narrator concludes by supposing she should have remained silent instead of pointing out the dangerous contradictions in the method of Miss Thornton, who believes that she works in the service of a noble purpose. To this noble purpose of reform, however, the narrator opposes her right to "refuse" in the face of her disillusionment. "Had I been bred in the last generation full of hope and unattainable desire I too would have declared that men and women are born equal but being of this generation with the colleges and professions open to me and able to learn that the other man is really stronger I say I will have none of it" (pp. 7-8).

Stein rejects, then, through her narrator's speech, the defenses of women's colleges which she had previously endorsed so wholeheartedly. She is now impatient with an education that would simply delegate women to a special sphere, an education that ultimately renders women as powerless and as ineffective as before. And yet the strategy with which she opposes women's education renders her own position contradictory and confusing.

In effect, her narrator's strategy epitomizes a major assumption of realism, the assumption that there is a level of reality which can be represented by straightforward language. Her narrator, for example, claims to see through a number of "noble sentiments"—the women's movement, reform in general, even "the noble sentiment of devotion to one's alma mater" (p. 6)—and argues that these are not simply delusions, but dangerous delusions. As our observant moral watchdog, her strategy has been to lift the veil of delusion away from the truth which has been concealed.

And the truth to be revealed in the case of the feminists, the narrator insists, is that beneath their insistence upon "sameness" are "fundamental facts of sex" which she wonders if "the new woman" will ever "relearn" (p. 4). These "fundamental facts" are never specified for us, but her speech clearly points to the way in which they are constituted by "real" categories of differences between men and women. And men represent the category by which women are to be judged. They are honorable, honest, just, active, and vital. All of the women imaged for us, on the other hand, from the guest of honor to the "woman in the rush for position" to Miss Thornton, derive their power not in open and honest confrontation but by doublespeak, surreptitiousness, and downright sneakiness. Although the "dishonorable" image of women is the precise opposite of the image advocated by those who defended educated womanhood as virtuous nurturers of society, by her strategy of seeing to the bottom of things, Stein's rhetorical argument has ultimately put her in the same camp with those who rhetorically defended women's education. And this was a camp whose initial assumption was that women occupied separate and special spheres.

If her narrator has succeeded in clarifying certain facts for herself, then Stein has only made use of this vehicle at the expense of obfuscating the nature of her own difficult position. For if fundamental facts are the basis of and constitute real sexual differences, which fundamental fact applies to her? It is clear that the narrator identifies herself with the "male ideal" which she uses as a standard of judgment. By insisting upon destroying what she sees as illusions, the narrator insists upon her own honesty, her integrity, and in terms of her own defi-

nition, her "maleness." And honesty is the logical extension of
her realistic attitude. Yet if the logic of realism delineates a
strategy by which she can maintain her own integrity, by the
end of the speech she is maintaining it by another means. She
is one of those "rare women" who "should say no" to reform, because she finds in her "heart" that she "needs must" (p. 8). Having consulted both the honesty of the male mind and the "rare"
sincerity of the female heart, Stein can only be reserving a special place for herself as an anomaly in terms of traditional categories.[12] She is a woman speaking as a man and by
appropriating this special position she has already called into
question the very terms of her own argument, and threatened
the very integrity she wanted so desperately to maintain. The
other choice, however, would have presented itself as even more
desperate. For if she had not created a special position for herself, her speech would have logically persuaded her to join "the
great mass of the world's women" who, she points out, "should
content themselves with attaining to womanhood," (pp. 5-6) and,
we could add, what Stein undoubtedly considered to be a trap of
silence.

In the narrative, whose subtitle is "Philip Redfern, Student
of the Nature of Women," Stein will continue to investigate
the nature of "womanhood." Interestingly, she does so within
the framework of a scandalous seduction which takes place at
a small women's college. Thus the question of womanhood is
situated in the larger framework of "propriety." In a manner
of speaking, however, before the narrative has even begun, the
sexual scandal has already taken place. For by not situating
herself in either of the categories which the "fundamental facts
of sex" would seem to designate as the only possible locations,
the narrator has already put into question "propriety" at least
in the initial sense of that word: "true nature." The necessities
of Stein's own position further propel her to question the very
framework that was meant to contain the solution.

II. Seduced by Speech

"The contradiction isn't in me," Adele said sitting up to the occasion and illustrating her argument by vigorous gestures, "it is in your perverted ideas." (Gertrude Stein, *Q.E.D.*)

In a sense, Stein had been seduced by speech. Rhetorical defenses of women's colleges may have been based, as Stein's was in 1898, upon an essential belief in a woman's "human traits" and her essential equality with men. Politically, however, they advocated an education which made sexual distinctions look like unalterable facts. If this position was politically necessary, it did affect the administration and shape of a woman's college life, and in attempting to criticize the administration of women's colleges Stein's own rhetoric in her *Fernhurst* polemic ultimately persuaded her to accept a political position as rock bottom fact. Stein gives us a glimpse of her discomfort with the implications of her *Fernhurst* polemic in a brief apology at the end of her speech. Her reader, she says, is probably "tired of this posing" (p. 8). It would seem, then, that Stein catches herself, as she had so often in *Q.E.D.*, in a false pose. However, in the interest of clarifying the situation for herself and maintaining a firm position, she follows this apology by insisting upon the necessity of speaking.

Her narrator's insistence upon speech can be seen as an extension of Adele's conclusions. At the end of *Q.E.D.* Adele represented speech as a sort of moral imperative. If Helen was wrong in her "whole duty of silence," Adele saw it as right and indeed as her duty to speak; for she assumed that speech was a transparent vehicle of explanation which, used in the right way, was capable of revealing "things as they are." Seeing speech as a moral imperative, however, entailed making certain moral distinctions between the way in which Mabel used language as a form of hypocrisy and deceit, and the way in which Adele used language, that is, openly, honestly, and clearly. By making speech into a moral imperative, however, Adele had already put into question the transparency and neutrality of language. For the ultimate goal of her moral imperative, speech, was a self-serving one: to maintain her integrity and coherence, first, by separating herself from Helen's "wrong" duty of silence, and finally by using it as a means of silencing her "immoral" competitor for Helen, Mabel. The issue, then, was not simply propriety, but also proprietorship, or who had the "right" to own Helen.

In this respect, it is interesting that the way in which the narrator of *Fernhurst* images feminists is reminiscent of the ways in which Mabel is imaged in the triangular affair of *Q.E.D.* The impulse to represent Mabel's position by converting it into that of the feminists, and particularly Miss Thornton's rather ominous position, meant that Stein's version of the Bryn Mawr affair has a significantly different outcome and emphasis. In the Bryn Mawr affair, Philip Hodder had seduced Mary Gwinn into leaving the college and marrying him. In *Fernhurst*, the college president, Miss Thornton, successfully retains Janet Bruce (Mary Gwinn's representative) at the college and ousts Philip Redfern (Hodder's representative) from his post. The relationship between the two women is maintained in Stein's novel, then, while Philip Redfern is left at loose ends. He deserts his wife, makes several unsuccessful attempts at a career, and gradually sinks into failure. Philip Redfern, then, like Adele in *Q.E.D.*, is not only a seeker of knowledge, but a lover who is ultimately defeated. Janet Bruce, like Helen in *Q.E.D.*, is essentially passive. Powerless to affect her own destiny, she simply becomes the object of rivalrous claims to ownership.

However, there is an important difference between the two books, for in *Fernhurst* there is not just one, but two triangular affairs. Stein provides herself with one source of analysis in the affair amongst Redfern, Janet Bruce, and Miss Thornton, while the relationship between Redfern and his wife, which is broken up by Janet Bruce, provides her with another. *Fernhurst*, then, is a doubled rendition of the triangular affair in *Q.E.D.*

This important difference has been ignored or evaded by commentators on the narrative who are simply interested in making exact equations between *Q.E.D.*, *Fernhurst*, and Stein's life. Leon Katz, for instance, says: "Hodder and Miss Gwinn were in the position Gertrude and May had been in, with Carey Thomas making up the third member of a triangle, just as Mabel Haynes had done."[13] Katz's version is not inaccurate, but his emphasis is interesting. Put differently, we could say that Gertrude was the intruder in the May Bookstaver-Mabel

Haynes relationship, just as Alfred Hodder was the intruder in the Carey Thomas-Mary Gwinn relationship. Katz dismisses the question of "ownership," of "stealing the property of another," which was an important issue in *Q.E.D.* and is again in *Fernhurst*. More importantly, perhaps, Katz does not follow the logic of his initial equation. Recognizing that Stein was in the position of Hodder, it would seem logical to say that she "identifies" herself with his representative in the novel, Philip Redfern. Nevertheless, when Katz comes to place her in the novel, he does so by saying that Stein identified with the deserted wife, Nancy, and used Woodrow Wilson for her model for Redfern.[14] Bridgman follows his lead by identifying Stein with Nancy.[15] Instead of recognizing her possible identification with a number of positions in the novel, this critical impulse would, so to speak, save Stein's integrity by placing her either in one position or the other. Thus, these critical positions and positionings not only evade the question of propriety (in all senses of the word) which the novel raises, but also the novel's more radical gestures in this connection. For the plot's central complication is precisely that most of the characters do not stay in their proper place.

On the most literal basis, this is evidenced by the way in which geography takes on important connotations in *Fernhurst*. Of all her characters, Stein's protagonist, Philip Redfern, is perhaps the most displaced in this regard. He is a Southerner who attends college in the Midwest, marries a Western woman, and comes to teach at an Eastern college. Each of these locations designates not just an outlook but a standard of conduct.

Because Redfern is from the South he is trained in elaborate chivalry which equips him with a polished and courteous guard. The "typical coeducational college of the Middle West" which he attends is a "sober-minded, earnest, moral, democratic community" (pp. 23-24). It is at this rather idyllic and chummy place that Philip meets the sober-minded, earnest, and democratic Nancy Talbot whose "simple and pure instincts" apparently suit her well for attaining her ideal of exact equality and comradeship with the men at the college. She counters Redfern's surprise that she had allowed a young boy friend to rest his head on her lap by telling him: "I am a Western woman

and believe in men's honesty and in my own." (p. 27). Philip,
whose instincts are more "dangerous and decadent," nevertheless allows himself to be swept away by this ideal. "You wonderful Western woman," Philip exclaims, "Surely you have made
a new world" (p. 27). Thinking that he has met his ideal woman,
Philip marries Nancy only to discover within two years that
his ideal "proved sufficiently inadequate to his needs" (p. 27).
When he arrives at the Eastern college to teach, on the other
hand, he finds the place more cultured, refined, and restrained.
At the tea where Philip meets Janet Bruce, people chat about
Swinburne, Pater, and James; Janet quotes a line in Greek
from the Iliad. Out of place in this refined atmosphere, Nancy
ineffectively expends her earnest energy trying to sort out her
confused feelings while watching Philip seduce Janet Bruce
with heady discussions of "naive realism" (p. 14). For Philip
once again thinks that he has met his ideal in the gentle and
refined intelligence of Janet Bruce.

As Philip drifts from place to place, no fixed standards guide
his action. Each place formulates certain ideals for him, but
his ideals, the narrator tells us, are in constant battle with his
instincts. This battle with his instincts is the result of Philip's
family life, and genealogy is another way in which the narrator
attempts to place her characters. Philip is the son of "ill-as-
sorted parents" whose rivalrous claims over him formulate his
character. The "strong emotional flavor of his mother's nature"
and her restless desire have the strongest influence over him;
and from his mother Philip gets his insatiable quest to know
and understand women. For the mother's "constant rebellion
against the pressure of her husband's steady domination found
effective expression in the training of her son to be the cham-
pion of the rights of women" (p. 22). His father, "a man determined always to be master in his own house" fails to notice
what is going on and simply "relied on Philip's manhood and
inherited quality to make him the man he would have him"
(p. 22). As the result of this mixed influence, Philip learns
"scrupulous courtesy and power of reserve" from his father but
not his "fixed standards" (p. 23). His principles are his mother's
and these are "of the nature of longings and aspirations rather
than of settled purpose" (p. 23).

Watching his parents battle, Philip becomes interested in studying the nature of marriage, but in the process he also repeats his parents' rivalry. In his marriage to Nancy he finds "it must be again an armed neutrality but this time it was not as with his parents an armed neutrality between equals but with an inferior who could not learn the rules of the game" (pp. 27-28). And the rivalry between his parents over Philip also foreshadows his own future rivalry with Miss Thornton over Janet Bruce. As a passive object of rivalrous claims, Philip occupied a position between his parents that will in turn be the position which Janet Bruce will come to occupy in the rivalry between Miss Thornton and Philip. In that contest, Philip's influence over Janet is much like his mother's influence over him, for he releases her repressed emotional life. Importantly, this influence is mutual, for Janet, albeit passively, offers him "exquisite knowledge" and Philip "never tired of meeting and knowing and devoting himself to any woman who promised to fulfill for him his desire" (p. 33). Miss Thornton's oppressive attitude, on the other hand, reminds us of his father's domineering attitude and his "cold reserve[,] his strong will and the perfect rectitude of his conduct" (p. 22). Janet's own history makes her the perfect object of rivalry between this new set of parents—for she is "unattached" and her own parents are dead. Her "place" is a sort of abstracted dream world which is only given "concrete form" by either Philip, who brings her back to, and relies upon, her emotional life and desire, or by Miss Thornton, who guides her "practical affairs."

Stein's analysis of Philip's family life, and her rendering of its repetition in his quest for an "ideal" woman, has the configurations of an oedipal drama. In the triangular affair of the narrative, authority and its power of repression reside not simply in the biological father or male, but in Miss Thornton, who occupies the place of the father. Janet, occupying the oppressed position of both mother and child, epitomizes the nature of this ill-defined locus in patriarchal society. Although the narrator seems to hold Miss Thornton's position in contempt, while she is practically as fascinated by and attracted to Janet's position as Philip is, neither position is valorized by the narrator who points out that they are both "immoral." In Janet's case, this seems to mean ineffective, for, totally indifferent to "worldly matters," she is incapable of directing her own life or seeing the ramifications of her actions. Miss Thornton, on the other hand, is a contradiction in terms. Stein's narrator explains both Miss Thornton's contradictory position and its immorality by placing her, as she had with Philip, in terms of Miss Thornton's family history.

Miss Thornton has descended from a line of women who both test and transgress the traditional bounds of womanhood. In the first generation of these women, Miss Thornton's great-grandmother, a Quaker, "kept strictly within the then womanly bounds" although she "carried to its utmost the then practical woman's life . . . its fervor of emotion and prayer, and its devout practical morality" (p. 15). Miss Thornton's grandmother "went outside of Quaker bounds," was known in "wider circles" and took part in "exaggerated religious enthusiasms" though she "never lost her sense of criticism and judgment" (pp. 15-16). Miss Thornton, who "found expression in still wider experience," dismissed the Quaker doctrines entirely, and found "her exaltation in Swinburne and Walter Pater" (p. 16). Although Miss Thornton is unaware of it, the narrator tells us, it is by her public reading of these poets that she exerts the strongest influence over her students. While the women in her ancestry managed to keep in touch with both their feelings and their ideals, Miss Thornton has lost touch with both. The narrator gives us the impression that this is because Miss Thornton has strayed too far away from the bounds of womanhood. For, although Miss Thornton has noble "male" ideals as founder and dean of the college, she is driven by a need to dominate others and she fails to see how this is in contradiction to her ideal. Thus, having lost touch with both her instincts and her ideal, Miss Thornton is immoral; "the quality of her conduct as an influence could never come to her" (p. 18).

Having delineated certain positions, with their attendant codes of conduct, the narrator renders the inadequacy of these positions and codes for assessment and interpretation. The seduction becomes a scandal because the two characters involved in it, Philip and Janet, can not see its effects, and the two characters involved in the ramifications of the affair, Miss

Thornton and Nancy, cannot even see it happening. Miss Thornton, guided by "expediency" and her "instinct for domination," simply makes certain assumptions about Janet Bruce, much in the same way that Philip's father had with Philip: "It was not that she did not see the passionate life in the reserved nature, but she who knew in herself how abstracted ecstasy could be never once thought that this passionate life could desire a concrete form" (p. 32). She was thus "too blinded by her strength and preconceptions to notice the variation in the manner of this pair who were continually with her" (p. 35). Nancy Redfern, too, is blinded by her preconceptions:

She could not escape the knowledge that something stronger than community of interest bound her husband and Miss Bruce together. She tried resolutely to interpret it all in Western terms of comradeship and greater intellectual equality never admitting for a moment the conception of a possible marital disloyalty a conception so foreign to the moral American mind. . . . These were things that were simply not done in coeducational middle western America (p. 39).

Janet Bruce, living in "a world of realised dreams" is totally unaware of the value of discretion, and Philip is blinded by his chivalry to the effects of his transgression:

They never looked forward content with the deepening knowledge of life and love and sex that each day brought them and Redfern felt in his chivalrous way that all desire that he roused in her mind it was his duty to fulfill and that no price could be too great to pay for the knowledge of her wondrous nature that she so freely gave him (p. 34).

Philip's real blind spot, however, is literally the result of excessive vision.

It was true that like many keen observers he was apt to credit others with more blindness than they possessed and to believe that what he saw must by virtue of his greater power of sight be hidden from lesser eyes and minds . . . (p. 34).

The narrator's commentary here seems to be an ironic evaluation of her own valorization of "keen observation" in her initial polemics against feminism. The ways in which each character represses an uneasy knowledge of the vulnerability and limitations of his or her own position seems to echo the narrator's own uneasiness. She says of Philip's position, for example:

Before the fact of others' understanding becomes completely felt there are always unconscious pricks and blows that prepare the skin for extra sensitiveness when the burning glass is at length applied. While no one yet has said they see we are dimly aware of uneasiness and fear (p. 34).

For Philip, in spite of "his strong delusion" of keener eyesight, could not be "entirely blind to the significant smiles and glances" from the students at the college. The students both see and exploit the affair:

It is not in the old and experienced that danger to secret and subtle relations lies, it is always harsh and crude young things who tear down the sacred veil and with bold eyes pry into the delicate souls and subtle meanings of their elders and translating them into their bald straight words laugh and dissect things their elders dare not see (p. 35).

The narrator reveals an ambivalent attitude toward the students' theatrics. The narrative itself repeats the students' act of voyeurism and performance, and significantly, just as the students mock Redfern and Bruce doing "naive realism," so too does the narrative celebrate and theatricize the seduction's release of repressed desire and knowledge, thereby subverting the form of realism meant to contain it. The students interpret the affair "at a distance," however, from a position that is in itself violent and that ultimately, as we shall see, does violence to the affair. Their "bold eyes" "pry into" and "tear down" sacred veils and they "misrepresent the delicacy and subtle meanings of their elders." The narrator, on the other hand, does not distance herself in the same way. She is in a sense both inside the affair and outside of it, creating sympathy both for the transgressors, Philip and Janet, and the betrayed and deserted wife, Nancy. Hence, how to evaluate and conclude her story becomes the narrator's explicit concern.

The French, the narrator tells us, "consider that in the usual grouping of two and an extra which humanity so constantly supplies it is the two that get something from it all who are of importance and whose claim should be considered" (p. 38)— this would be Philip and Janet. The Americans, on the other hand, "accustomed to waste happiness and be reckless of joy find morality more important than ecstasy and the lonely extra of more value than the happy two" (p. 38)—Nancy's position. Having delineated these two possibilities, the narrator does not really decide between them. The triangle involving Janet, Philip, and Nancy, then, presents the narrator with a different possibility for interpretation. In grouping the three together in the beginning of the story, the narrator comments that "It was a group that would have puzzled the most practiced of interpreters" (p. 12). All three are in powerless positions, and since all of their claims are equally deserving of her sympathy, the narrator can establish no hierarchy of judgment. The narrator ultimately leaves the choice up to two spectators, a man and his wife discussing the affair, and through them, the reader. The man defends Philip as "a wonderful man," clever and brilliant, whose talents are going to waste. The wife, siding with Nancy, thinks that Philip deserves his fate as a failure for having treated Nancy so badly. Subsuming the battle of interpretation into a typical scenario between husband and wife, the narrator indicates that the process of interpretation, a battle of wills in which judgment depends upon a self-serving position, could itself be endless.

Having made interpretation contingent upon will, Stein concludes her novel with Miss Thornton, whose will to dominate effectively forecloses all possibilities at least on one scene, her college. Significantly, it is the students' theatrics, those "crude" misrepresentations of the "subtle meanings of their elders" that initiate the measures that destroy the affair. In the very act of publicizing the affair, the students instigate the release of that uneasy knowledge that those involved in the affair had feared but repressed, and by doing so, they provoke the repressive measures that bring about the affair's conclusion. Just as the students cause Philip to become uneasily aware of his own position of vulnerability, they also succeed in confirming Miss Thornton's worst fears. "Very likely," the narrator tells us, "it would not have been long before Miss Thornton herself would have noted the disturbed mind and roused feeling of her housemate and constant companion," but "her eyes are opened" when she overhears two students who have espied Philip and Janet together and are mocking them. Miss Thornton takes "one long look" at the two together, "sees" the affair, and begins to plot to end it (pp. 36-37).

Realizing the ineffectiveness of directly confronting the two involved, she decides to play on Nancy's jealousy. She informs Nancy that her husband is the subject of "scandalous talk," thereby confirming Nancy's own suspicions. Miss Thornton "had made a certainty of what Mrs. Redfern had regarded as an impossibility" (p. 42). Awakened to a new possibility that she had half-realized herself, Nancy debates how she is to confirm this new insight, to "see" the evidence for herself. Though "deeply ashamed of the means she must pursue," Nancy brings the affair to an end by the dishonorable act of reading Philip's private letters. Moreover, when confronted by Philip, who catches her in the act, she commits the further dishonorable deed of lying about her reasons.

The conclusion of the affair, then, is brought about by "dishonorable" means. Nancy and Miss Thornton both resort to indirectness and surreptitiousness, thus repeating and demonstrating the actions of the feminists whom the narrator so firmly castigated in her introductory polemic. In the course of concluding her narrative, however, the narrator has become more ambivalent about these "dishonorable" characters and their methods. If the narrator sympathizes with Nancy's struggle with the dishonorable methods she deploys to conclude the affair, the narrator has also become more sympathetic with Miss Thornton's methods, which reveal a "deep wisdom" (p. 41). Indeed this concession to Miss Thornton is necessary, for if her methods are dishonorable they are also effective. And to be effective in the terms of this novel means that the logic of the narrator's own strategy of realism takes over with a kind of fatal momentum and inevitability. For having successfully plotted to bring the affair to an end, Miss Thornton expels the disrupter, Philip, from the college, gradually manages to squelch any student gossip that would perpetuate knowledge about the affair, and retains Janet Bruce in her "very same place" (p. 49). In doing so, Miss Thornton becomes the executor of Stein's own strategy of realism, a genre which, as Leo Bersani points out, "served nineteenth-century society by providing it with strategies for containing and repressing its disorder."[16]

Stein indicates her dissatisfaction with the integrity she had attained, however, by rendering Miss Thornton's "propriety" effective but hollow, her order the mockery of moral order. Stein's critique of this arch-rival feminist's strategy and her own, then, has been that by acquiring power in society through these strategies women simply succeed in conserving a simulacrum of the social order that had formerly served to repress them. Janet Bruce, whose "wondrous nature" is potentially the source of "exquisite knowledge," remains silent and passive to the end and is reappropriated back within a repressive framework. By analogy, Helen has been handed back to Mabel, May to Mabel Haynes, and in the very act of speaking Stein has silenced herself. The internal contradictions of maintaining a realistic position, as her next novel, *Three Lives*, further demonstrates, were becoming increasingly intolerable to her. A different way of speaking and a different framework were needed. Although Philip, who is capable of giving Janet's potential "concrete form," is Stein's alternative to Miss Thornton, he is ineffective because the terms of this novel are unable to generate an adequate formula to express and contain desire: "In this life as in all his human relations his instincts gave the lie to his ideals and his ideals to his instincts" (p. 47). Thus he is left to wander from place to place, "failing everywhere" and as effectively expelled from the novel as he was ousted from the college. He will reappear again, however, in *Three Lives*, his character merged with the character of another wanderer and seeker of knowledge, Melanctha. And in this story Stein will attempt once again to reinterpret her affair from a different position and with a different voice.

III

Three Lives—Three Deaths

A thing which has not been understood inevitably reappears; like an unlaid ghost, it cannot rest until the mystery has been solved and the spell broken. (Sigmund Freud)

Quoting even oneself lacks a flavor of reality.(Gertrude Stein, *Q.E.D.*)

Three Lives was the first of her novels Gertrude Stein considered suitable for publication. This novel is a much more discreet re-presentation of her triangular affair and the issues of power and desire it had raised. In *Q.E.D.* and *Fernhurst*, she had indiscreetly relied upon recognizable people and events for the vehicle of her story. In *Three Lives* she relies upon her observations of the more obscure lives of one of her own servants and of the blacks she had treated as a medical student in Baltimore. The sexuality pervading the novel is carefully euphemistic; the lesbian affair of *Q.E.D.* is converted into the heterosexual affair of the "Melanctha" story and into numerous, though marginal and platonic "romances" between women.

Despite these precautions, the manuscript was rejected by established publishing houses. In the opinion of the readers at Robert Merrill, the subject matter was *too* obscure to demand the elaborate attention she paid it: "A miniature," she was informed, "can be overdone."[1] There was a more universal basis of rejection, however. While attending to one consideration of literary decorum—what is said—Stein neglected to gauge the

effect of her break with the other dictum of literary propriety—
how it is said. Dismissing the self-conscious "literary" language
she had used to depict the educated classes of her first two
novels, Stein attempted in this novel to render the lives of two
German immigrant women and one mulatto in the language
of their own dialects. This experiment met with the objection
that her writing contained too many "foreignisms" and was
ungrammatical and illiterate. Stein was so determined to see
her novel in print, however, that after three years of persistence
through failure, she finally brought out the novel through a
vanity press, paying $660 for the publication of five hundred
copies.

This degree of ownership over her novel afforded Stein the
privilege of staunchly refusing to listen to her editor's pleas
that she correct the grammar. However, she did listen to his
advice that she change the title from *Three Histories* to *Three
Lives*. Her editor felt that "Three Histories" would confuse her
novel with his "real historical publications";[2] Stein perhaps had
an inchoate intuition, one that she would later refine more
programmatically, that she was more interested in "existence,"
or the duration of a "continuous present" than in history's chronology of remembered significant events.

Stein's subject matter—the seemingly insignificant lives of
three illiterate women—lent itself well to the subversion of the
novel's reliance upon the conventions of history and to the
exploration of her alternative concept of "existence." For the
meaning of these women's lives could not be formulated or
explained by a narrative history's teleology, but rather seemed
to evade its grasp. Not only is their social status marginal—
Anna and Lena's as immigrant servants, and Melanctha's as
an anomalous mulatto—but their lives remain insistently marginal, incapable of assimilation into a coherent structure capable of explaining the significance of their destinies. For all
of Anna's tremendous exertion of will, her proud conquests,
won only in "the name of" her employers, remain minor to the
point of triviality. More importantly, the price Anna pays for
having a great deal of will but no legitimate way of exerting
it, is to release it upon herself and to become, finally, a self-
destructive whirlwind of activity. Melanctha's hard-earned

"wisdom," gained by steadily moving beyond the guideposts of memory and purpose, is hardly a source of survival. Giving free rein to her wandering desire in search of something she cannot name, Melanctha is finally left "lost" in a world that "went whirling in a mad weary dance around her."[3] Lena, inertly submitting to doing only what is expected of her, is not assimilated into the life of her society by marriage and childbirth, but instead comes closer and closer to death with each new life she gives. The "meaning" of Stein's characters' lives is not revealed but lost in their abrupt deaths, which go unremarked and unmourned.

Since these characters are incapable of assimilation into their society, or, in a sense, into their own narrative histories, Stein's novel poses the question of how appropriate propriety is without property. It is both poignant and ironic that these women try so hard to be good characters—"good" in *Three Lives* translating into a sense of socially accepted propriety. These servant women "know" their "proper places" but the more they seem to want to act from them the more they really fail to do so. Instead, they are caught up within an inexplicable and inexorable momentum that destroys them. This momentum is so destructive that it makes Stein's epigraph for *Three Lives* seem like an understatement: "And so I am an unhappy one and it is neither my fault nor life's." But her inability to "explain" unbalances the traditional novel's structure, for "the meaning of life," as Walter Benjamin points out, "is really the center about which the novel moves."[4] Instead of centering her novel through explanation, Stein's narrator is as inarticulate and "illiterate" as her characters, immersing us in these women's lives rather than giving us a perspective on them. Their "existences" are rendered through a narrative that seems to endure, rather than to gain significance through the accumulation of dramatic event. Stylistically, this is achieved through the increasingly consistent use of the present participle, particularly in the "Melanctha" story, and repetitious refrains that bring us back every time we seem to move forward. Stein was later to label this immersion into the duration of a dramatically flattened moment the "continuous present" and to recognize the innovative style of *Three Lives* as her first step into the twentieth century.

Two early critics of *Three Lives* immediately saw the potential of Stein's subject matter to bring about a stylistic revolution. At one extreme Wyndham Lewis included *Three Lives* in his tirade against modernism in general:

... in adopting the simplicity, the illiterateness of the mass average of the Melanctha's and Anna's, Miss Stein gives proof of all the false revolutionary propagandist *plainmanism* of her time. The monstrous desperate soggy *lengths* of primitive life are undoubtedly intended as an epic contributing to the present mass democracy.[5]

Richard Wright, on the other hand, praised *Three Lives* for the very qualities that led Lewis to denigrate it. An ardent Communist, Richard Wright wrote that to counter rumors that Stein was a decadent hashish smoker in Paris with no "proletarian sympathies" he conducted the successful experiment of reading "Melanctha" to a group of illiterate black dock-workers. They responded immediately with appreciative understanding and his faith in Stein's writing was restored.[6]

More recent critics have generally favored stylistic analyses that rely largely upon compositional analogies made to the radically innovative techniques of the painters with whom Stein was beginning to associate, and are derived from Stein's own later dramatization of the creation of *Three Lives*. As Stein later told the story, she was inspired to break with convention in *Three Lives* by her task of translating Flaubert's *Trois Contes* and by her study of Cezanne's portrait of his wife which she sat beneath while writing. "Everything I have done was influenced by Flaubert and Cezanne, and this gave me a new feeling about composition,"[7] Stein was to proclaim, conveniently ignoring in the "everything" her first two novels, which were definitely not influenced by Cezanne or Flaubert. In specifying the nature of this influence, Stein draws an analogy between her art and Cezanne's that seems apt; the description of the decentered and democratic style of *Three Lives* is captured in the description of her understanding of Cezanne's painting:

Up to that time composition had consisted of a central idea, to which everything else was an accompaniment and separate but not an end in itself, and Cezanne conceived the idea that in composition one thing was as important as another thing. Each part is as important as the whole, and that impressed me enormously and it impressed me so much that I began to write *Three Lives* under this influence and this idea of composition . . .[8]

Though the analogy is apt, this proclamation is staged in a way that her writing could not have been. But it is understandable as a strategy for appropriating legitimacy, for grounding her experiments in the experimental work done by self-conscious stylists who by the time of this statement had become acknowledged "fathers of twentieth-century art." However, the advantage of Stein's consistently proclaimed alliance with Cezanne, Picasso, Matisse and other painters has ultimately proved to be just as much a disadvantage, and understanding her work in the light of these artists, insufficient. Not only did Stein's proclaimed alliance give rise to the still tenacious image of a woman artist "created" by Cubism but it also led to the misunderstanding that Stein was opportunistic and her later, more radical writing was the "error" of essentially attempting to paint with her pen.[9] Often inept analogies have been substituted for more careful stylistic analyses of her language. The "repetitive sentences" of *Three Lives*, one critic tells us, are "like each exacting, carefully negotiated plane" of Cezanne's picture, "each one building up, phrase by phrase the substance of her characters."[10] And the "continuous present," another tells us, "like the formal analysis of Cezanne and the experiments of Picasso which were soon to lead to the first Cubist pictures, . . . was a means of holding the object or the statement out of time for the purpose of discovering its 'reality'."[11] These statements give the impression that Stein sat before Cezanne's painting carefully translating mass, light, and color into words, phrases, and syntax, and reveal how cautious one must be in evaluating the nature of the influence of Stein's growing participation in the radical movement in the arts on her work.

What Stein undoubtedly gained through her association with this group of painters was the support to push beyond the dictates of convention. As her first two novels indicate, Stein was inclined toward unconventional and even scandalous subject matter anyway—although she was not interested and certainly not comfortable in exploiting it as such. If anything, she was interested in stating her unconventional subject in the terms of a conventionally acceptable mode of realism. The painters with whom she was beginning to associate, on the other hand, took the conventional subjects of painting and rendered them scandalous by freeing representation from the conventional requirements of "realistic" description. Viewers at the 1905 Salon d'Automne were outraged by the vivid splashes of color with which Matisse rendered his *Woman with the Hat* and attempted to scratch "the ugly smears of paint" off with their fingernails. Gertrude's brother Leo purchased the painting; and the artists meanwhile enjoyed the joke that the model, Mme. Matisse, was dressed all in black and seated against a white wall.[12] Picasso's portrait of Gertrude Stein, for which she posed at the time she was writing *Three Lives*, is indebted to his study of Cezanne and African sculpture for its break with traditional perspective. When the portrait met with the horrified objection that "she does not look like it," Picasso calmly replied "but she will." However, Stein only gradually came to terms with the problems of conventional representation by working through them in her own medium. Meanwhile, she both throve upon the scandalous atmosphere the painters were generating and appropriated its shock value, happily reporting to a friend immediately after the completion of *Three Lives* that her mildly salacious novel was a "noble combination"—not of Flaubert and Cezanne—but of "Swift and Matisse."[13]

In naming the "fathers" of her art, Stein's consistent pairing of author and painter indicate that she never lost sight of the literary nature of her experiment. However, she never expanded upon how either Swift or Flaubert specifically influenced her, and it is difficult to see any clear stylistic relationships. The gentle irony of her stories only dimly echoes the harsher satire of *The Tale of the Tub*, which she was reading at the time, and although the good Anna in some ways resembles Flaubert's silent, thrifty, and illiterate servant Felicité in *Trois Contes*, stylistically, Flaubert's impersonal and articulate narrator is directly opposed to Stein's narrator who immerses herself in the language and lives of her characters in *Three Lives*. It is interesting, too, that Stein made this appeal to the stylistic precision of the "connoisseur of the 'mot juste' " at a time when she found it necessary to defend the deliberate seriousness of her art against accusations that she was surrealistically exploiting the unconscious.[14]

Though retrospective compositional analogies to Stein's supposed influences are often apt in terms of placing her as a modernist, the contrast between Flaubert's perspective and Stein's on similar subject matter suggests that it could be just as fruitful to focus upon their differences. Flaubert's proclaimed goal was to turn the nineteenth-century novel away from "personal emotions and nervous susceptibilities" and to "endow it with the pitiless method, with the exactness of the physical sciences."[15] Mimicking the methodology of the physical sciences meant increased dependence upon empirical observation, upon visualizing every element so that the story expressed itself through what could be seen with clarity and exactitude. One of Flaubert's contributions to the modern novel, Alan Spiegel tells us, was that the "omniscient and god-like narrator was replaced by the seeing eye of man."[16]

In *Trois Contes*, Flaubert dramatizes the emotion of his character Felicité by reporting what she sees and describing the details of these scenes. When Virginie dies, for example, Felicité expresses her sorrow by going into Virginie's room every morning to "look around it" and recount to herself in visual detail each of her habitual acts in caring for the young girl. Her most passionate experience, a religious one, is dramatized by what she sees at her niece's first communion:

All through the Mass her heart was in her mouth. One side of the choir was hidden from her by M. Bourais, but directly opposite her she could see the flock of maidens, looking like a field of snow with their white crowns perched on top of their veils, and she recognized her little darling from a distance by her dainty neck and her rapt attitude. The bell tinkled. Every head bowed low, and there was silence. Then, to the thunderous accompaniment of the organ, choir and congregation joined in singing the *Agnus Dei*. Next, the boys' procession began, and after that the girls got up from their seats. Slowly, their hands joined in prayer, they went towards the brightly lit altar, knelt on the first step, received the Host one by one, and went back to their places in the same order. When it was Virginie's turn, Felicité leant forward to see her, and in one of those imaginative flights born of real affection, it seemed to her that she herself was in the child's place. Virginie's face became her own, Virginie's dress clothed her, Virginie's heart was beating in her breast; and as she closed her eyes and opened her mouth, she almost fainted away.[17]

Flaubert imagines his character as building up her powerfully vicarious experience cinematically, by the accumulative observation of visual details. However, Felicité's attempts to make the absent present, to understand things she cannot comprehend by seeing them, are shown to be both highly effective and extremely limited. They are effective because they produce a powerfully comforting illusion, as when Felicité attempts to understand the Holy Ghost by imagining what he looks like and finally taking great comfort in believing him to be her stuffed parrot. Thus does Flaubert capture both the poignancy of her emotion and the absurdity of Felicité's—and his own—reliance upon sight.

Informed perhaps by her own training in the physical sciences, Stein's first two novels reveal that she too believed in the certainty of proofs gained by seeing clearly. But these novels also indicate, particularly in *Fernhurst*, where excessively keen vision is a disadvantage rather than an advantage, her growing dissatisfaction with relying exclusively upon sight. It is perhaps significant that the good Anna so frequently breaks her eyeglasses, especially when she is most frustrated, for she is living in a world that is too murky to be "seen" clearly. If the modern novel moved away from an omniscient narrator to the "seeing eye of man," Stein begins in *Three Lives* to involve her readers by appealing less to their sense of sight than to their sense of hearing. The narrator of *Three Lives* not only increasingly relies upon rendering the story through dialogue, but both the characters' and the narrator's voice achieve emphasis by establishing a rhythm that carries with it palpable feeling:

And so Melanctha began once more to wander. It was all now for her very different. It was never rougher men now that she talked to, ahd she did not care much now to know white men of the, for her, very better classes. It was now something realler that Melanctha wanted, something that would fill her fully with the wisdom that was planted now within her, and that she wanted badly, should really wholly fill her.

Felicité could never have described the experience of her niece's first communion in the same way as Flaubert did, though we supposedly see the same things she sees. When Melanctha wanders, on the other hand, what she sees is less important than the insistence of her feelings rendered in a simpler language closer to that of Melanctha's.

Flaubert's dependence upon sight both questions and relies upon the extent to which western epistemology itself relies upon vision and metaphors of vision. However, one of Spiegel's suggestions about Flaubert's major novel implies that the scientifically objective status of observation is compromised by the desire of the observer. The scandal of *Madame Bovary*, Spiegel remarks, may have been provoked because through the visual detail of his language Flaubert takes us closer than any other author before him to the body of a woman.[18] The epistemological revolution of Melanctha would be that not only is Melanctha's knowledge, her "wisdom," so blatantly generated by her desire, but also that in *Three Lives* women are heard rather than seen; the rhythmic cadence of their thoughts and feelings take precedence over their visualization.

Traditionally, women have been both spoken for and seen, transformed into images designed for the reassurance and pleasure of the male spectator. Significantly, the paintings which Stein deemed most influential to her were all portraits of women. But Stein was not simply following the painters' lead as they explored new possibilities of expression by beginning with the most classical subject of portraiture, women. For Stein was in a different position. Just as Picasso was painting her, absorbing her identity into his identity as an artist, she was rewriting her story about May Bookstaver, her first lover. Though she had believed herself to be outside "the dark continent," posing as a male observer who was a student of the nature of women, she was also inside it, the subject of observation and portraiture herself. That in her third rewriting of this story the emphasis is more upon Melanctha, May's representative, than upon her lover Jeff, is an indication, perhaps, of Stein's growing identification with May's position. In *Three Lives*, Stein questions the limitation of women as a subject to be spoken for, and in posing the question begins to transgress those limits. The question becomes, not how does one speak for women, but how can they speak for themselves?

The first story of *Three Lives* is the most traditional of the three, but it is also the most ironic, posing the contradictions and limitations of the very concept of "tradition" through its character "The Good Anna." When Anna emigrates from Germany to the United States she carries with her a "firm old world sense of what was the right way for a girl to do" (p. 24) and her stubborn standards of thrift, of good and bad, of how to dress, of what to eat and how to address one's employers never change. Anna knows her place, or more importantly, she thinks she does. However, her "old world sense" is not only inadequate to her new country and a constantly changing world, but her inflexibility also becomes a measure of the destructiveness of adhering with unmitigated certainty to one's predefined place. For with all the force of her tremendous will power behind her misplaced idealism, Anna destroys herself by creating and striving to fulfill an image of her own character based upon these old world standards. "She worked away her appetite, her health and strength and always for the sake of those who begged her not to work so hard. To her thinking, in her stubborn, faithful, german soul, this was the right way for a girl to do" (p. 32).

Ironically, the very same will which gives her the resolve to create her own character also generates her impulse to control, even to "create" others. Alas for the foolish, the flirtatious, the sluggard, the spendthrift, or the melancholy when they come under Anna's stern command, for they are not allowed to indulge in their frivolity for long. But neither are her obese and passive mistresses whose lives exist like so much unkneaded bread for the more definitive Anna to shape. Given the means to direct her energies into a larger public realm, Anna would have made a fine general, but as a servant and a woman, she brings the level of political struggle down to domesticity. Every household she serves in becomes a battlefield. Her various "battles"—getting the best bargains, keeping the good dogs from the bad dogs, controlling the underservants—make her life "arduous and troubled" (p. 13). And well they might, for the contradiction in Anna's life—arising from knowing the proper meekness of her place and yet being incapable of maintaining it—is that although she has no authority she is constantly trying to exert it, and though she has no power, she is constantly trying to exercise it.

Anna's oppressive zeal reminds one of Miss Thornton, and "The Good Anna," so painful in some respects, in others seems to be Stein's playful parody of both herself and her second novel, *Fernhurst*. Many readers have recognized that the character of Miss Mathilda, an obese young woman who indulges in spontaneous purchases of oil paintings, hearty meals after long walks and periodic trips to Europe, is a caricature of Stein herself. Stein treats herself deprecatingly as a weak and timid mistress easily bowled over by the shrill Anna, but even more significantly as a "rebel with the cheerful Lizzies, the melancholy Mollies, the rough old Katies and the stupid Sallies" (p. 23). This caricature sets up a complex relationship of authority and an ironic attitude towards it. Anna has no real power but tries to gain it by "speaking through" Miss Mathilda. This, however, is ineffective, for Miss Mathilda, timid, hesitant, and secretly identifying with the rebels she must reprimand, is ultimately incapable of exerting any authority at all. If Stein identified with Miss Thornton's role of authority in the conclusion of *Fernhurst* she is clearly distancing herself from that role in *Three Lives* by her hesitance in speaking for others and by the parody of Miss Thornton that her character Anna represents.

All of Miss Thornton's activities are parodied by Anna's, though Anna's take place on a smaller scale and in a smaller realm. Both see themselves as educative authorities who must attempt to control the lives of a younger generation. However, if Miss Thornton finds her position as Dean a more dependable source of authority, Anna rarely finds it efficacious to appeal to her position as older and wiser. Both women ignore the paradox that "their ideal is in contradiction to their instinct": Miss Thornton contradicts her ideal of self-government for the college and Anna her more humble ideal of "what a good girl should do" by a will to dominate. Just as Miss Thornton maintains the propriety of her college by expelling the adulterous offender, so the good Anna, with her "high ideals for canine chastity and discipline," must keep the good dogs from the bad dogs. And Anna is just as adept as Miss Thornton at creating fictions to keep up dignified appearances. When Anna's dog Peter—"the spoiled good looking young man of her middle age" (p. 68)—commits the offense of impregnating the neighbor's dog Foxy, Anna convinces Foxy's owners that Peter is innocent though she knows he's not. Ultimately all of the contradictions which were implicit in Miss Thornton's position are made explicit by Anna's status as a servant. If Miss Thornton succeeds in establishing propriety only at the expense of serving the society which oppressed her, this is literally the case with Anna.

Both women remain unaware of this paradox by suppressing their knowledge of it. Basically they are in the same position as those they would control, and they themselves must resort to subterfuge and rebellion, just as they create the need for it on the part of those they would dominate. If Sally sneaks an occasional banana for her boyfriend, Anna is shrewd enough to catch her at it. If Melancholy Molly rebels by not conforming to Anna's wishes, Anna can send her away to work in a factory. Weakened by the experience, Molly returns to Anna pliant to her wishes. Anna's system of subterfuge, however, is more elaborate and draws its strength from the skill with which Anna creates fictions both for herself and others. She authorizes these fictions by a combination of establishing a network of friends and "conquering in the name of Miss Mathilda." In this manner, no one catches her when she gets a "steal" on prices:

The strictest of one price stores found that they could give things for a little less when the good Anna had fully said that "Miss Mathilda" could not pay so much and she could buy it cheaper "by Lindheims" (p. 11).

Actually, of course, the weak and timid Miss Mathilda would probably pay the regular price, and she could also afford it. Anna's thriftiness becomes an end in itself that is not even efficacious. The more money she saves by her bargaining, the more money Miss Mathilda has to "waste" on oil paintings. And the more carefully Anna saves her own money, the more it slips away from her in donations to the poor or in loans, never repaid, to the friends she relies upon. The most important and most devastating fiction Anna creates for herself is that she is in control. Though she gets a bargain, Anna somehow always has to pay the price.

Anna also manages to create the illusion of control for herself by deliberately seeking out the weakest, most easily guided women and men to work for. "Anna's superiors must be always these large helpless women, or be men, for none others could give themselves to be made so comfortable and free" (p. 25). Anna can be in control by taking care of those who seem to feel it their right to be taken care of.

Because of this strategy Anna finds herself in direct conflict with younger women as they all, in oedipal fashion, compete to please those who hold the place of the father:

She naturally preferred the boys, for boys love always better to be done for and made comfortable and full of good eating, while in the little girl she had to meet the feminine, the subtle opposition, showing so early in a young girl's nature (25).

Miss Wadsmith's niece, Jane, is the most troublesome in this regard. Ironically, Anna finds that she must do battle with Jane because Jane has used one of Anna's own strategies—calling upon Miss Wadsmith's name and non-existent authority to order Anna to do something. Anna revolts not because of the work Jane's order involves but because the order comes from Jane. When Jane marries and becomes the mistress, Anna simply leaves. For a while then, Anna can control her fate and she succeeds in repressing the knowledge that although she is a servant her impulse is to be the mistress. Like Miss Thornton, Anna's instinct and the knowledge she represses are ultimately more important to her than her consciously stated knowledge of what a good girl should do.

However, Anna's pretenses and illusions are more vulnerable to her position and to the explosive force of all that she represses than Miss Thornton's. Anna's repressed energy reveals itself in her physical appearance and her manner. Her body and bearing are often "stiff with repression," her "mouth drawn and firm," her lower jaw "strained with the upward pressure of resolve" (p. 28). In her battle with Miss Wadsmith's niece Miss Jane, Anna confronts Miss Wadsmith, her "bearing full of the strange coquetry of anger and of fear, the stiffness, the bridling, the suggestive movement underneath the rigidness of forced control, all the queer ways the passions have to show themselves all one" (p. 29).

Anna's most trying times are when she has to speak for what she wants, for then all the pressure and tension of her repressed energy is in direct conflict with her feeling of the impropriety of demanding anything. The conflict of these emotions renders her stiff, pale, and silent, but her potentially explosive silences ultimately emerge only in sharp jerky phrases which are inarticulate and incomprehensible to her listeners. When Anna speaks to Miss Wadsmith, finally it is the power of her mood which speaks for her: "Her words had not the strength of meaning they were meant to have, but the power in the mood of Anna's soul frightened and awed Miss Mary through and through" (p. 29).

The power of her moods are not always so effective. More usually she relies upon the power of her friends. These friendships give force to her words and serve as the basis for her speaking, as when she scolds those who mistreat animals and intimidates them because everyone knew that all the policemen on the beat were her friends. Or, when Anna wants to leave Miss Wadsmith she simply has her friend, the calmer and more efficient Mrs. Lehntman, speak for her. For when Anna herself attempts to address Miss Wadsmith, she cannot win her struggle to be "unfeeling, self-righteous and suppressed" (p. 35) and she leaves her mistress puzzled and uncomprehending.

This ground for speaking ultimately proves its own ground-

lessness to the good Anna, however. The more subtle contradiction of deriving her own authority from the nonauthority of
her mistresses is one she can successfully ignore. But the pitfall
of relying upon her friends is epitomized by her relationship
with Mrs. Lehntman, who is the major "romance in her life."
Like many of Anna's employers, Mrs. Lehntman is lazy and
careless, and out of her impulse to dominate and her desire to
please, Anna manages Mrs. Lehntman's life. But when Mrs.
Lehntman doesn't want to follow Anna's advice she simply
doesn't listen and the more dependent Anna is upon Mrs.
Lehntman, the less dependable Mrs. Lehntman becomes. "Mrs.
Lehntman was more willing to risk Anna's loss, and so the
good Anna grew always weaker in her power to control" (p.
54). At this point, the narrator explains that friendship is not
as secure a source of power as Anna has made it out to be:

Friendship goes by favor. There is always danger of a break or of a
stronger power coming in between. Influence can only be a steady
march when one can surely never break away (pp. 54-55).

This statement capsulates the reasons why Anna loses power
in each relationship she thought she controlled: Jane breaks
into her control over Miss Wadsmith's life, the doctor's wife
breaks up Anna's control over Dr. Shonjen, and Miss Mathilda
leaves to go to Europe. Those whom she thought she controlled
ultimately control her. Anna's influence could never "be a steady
march" because her illusion of power is contingent upon the
most insecure ground possible: her servitude. When Miss Mathilda leaves for Europe, Anna gives up playing power games
in employer-employee relationships and attempts to run a
boarding house. Even so, Anna continues to play her role as
the good servant. Without her employers however, who both
restrained her and gave her a framework of support, Anna's
repressed energy is released in a whirlwind of self-destructive
activity as she attempts both to please and manage the lives
of a whole boarding house full of people.

"The Good Anna" both parodies and goes beyond *Fernhurst*.
At the conclusion of *Fernhurst* Miss Thornton's moral order is
shown to be a mockery of morality, but it is effective and she

is left in control. Anna's control over her own life, however, increasingly slips away from her like the money she attempts to save with tight-fisted economy. "The Good Anna" reveals the failure of both will and propriety. If the exertion of will and control is a basic requirement for the formulation of propriety and character, the more Anna strives to create her "character" the more she herself fades away. Her life, rather than being a "progression," is a recession, and her death seems to represent the ultimate erosion of her "character" in the face of events she increasingly cannot control. And the story, the framework which "brings her to life," simply recounts her decline and death. In "The Good Anna" Stein's servitude has radical consequences for the literary formulation of "character" itself.

Stein extends this inquiry in the story "Melanctha." Unlike the more definitive Anna, Melanctha is enigmatic: "She was always full with mystery and subtle movements and denials and vague distrusts and complicated disillusions" (p. 89). Melanctha meets each of Anna's qualities, then, with their opposite: for Anna's assertiveness, Melanctha has denials, for Anna's trust, Melanctha has only distrust, for Anna's illusions, Melanctha has disillusions that are "vague" and "complicated," full of mystery, and incapable of expression. Unlike Anna, Melanctha has no set position, no stable place to operate from because she is caught up in a ceaseless, restless need to wander. These wanderings are propelled by Melanctha's search for "wisdom," a euphemism for knowledge about sexuality and power, and guided by the contradictions and vicissitudes of her desire. Melanctha is very much like one of the characters Miss Thornton would have expelled or Anna would have tried to reform— the rebels with whom Mathilda secretly identified.

It is not that Melanctha does not want to be "good" like Anna, or that she does not seek the "right position," which she sees as marriage. The force of her desire, however, constantly overwhelms her. In contrast to her friend Rose who adheres with strict compliance to what she deems "proper conduct," the "complex desiring Melanctha" is incapable of making "her life all simple like Rose Johnson. ... Melanctha was always losing what she had in wanting all the things she saw" (p. 89).

It is significant that Melanctha's story begins with her relationship to Rose. Melanctha, like so many of Stein's "rebels,"
is in complete submission to an overpowering and domineering
woman and her mock propriety. Thus, the framework of power
relations once again both formulates and contains the enigma
of character: who is Melanctha and what does she want? "Why
did the subtle, intelligent, attractive, half-white girl Melanctha
Herbert love and do for and demean herself in service to this
coarse, decent, sullen, ordinary black childish Rose and why
was this immoral, promiscuous, shiftless Rose married, while
Melanctha with her white blood and attraction and her desire
for a right position had not yet been really married" (p. 86).
Even though this question is posed at the outset of Melanctha's
story, her relationship with Rose is one of the last relationships
in her life. The conflation of beginning and ending guarantees
that the story will not in fact give us the clue or key to Melanctha's motivation and therefore her character. Instead, the
story becomes the performance of this character motivated by
an unnameable desire which struggles within and disrupts the
conventional literary framework that formulates it. Melanctha
is unique among Stein's women characters in that the force of
her sexuality more insistently disrupts the framework of propriety and control.

If Melanctha's story begins and ends with her submission to
Rose, her "wanderings" are initiated in rebellion to her father,
an "unendurable" and domineering black man whose power
Melanctha nonetheless respects. "Melanctha had a strong respect for any kind of successful power. It was this that always
kept Melanctha nearer, in her feeling toward her virile and
unendurable black father, than she ever was in her feeling for
her pale yellow, sweet-appearing mother. The things she had
in her of her mother, never made her feel respect" (p. 96).
Melanctha's first sexual stirrings are euphemistically represented by her love of horses and John the coachman's growing
attraction to the "power in her of a woman." Her father becomes
angry when John reveals his attraction to Melanctha. After
challenging the coachman to a fight which Melanctha's father
loses, he angrily attempts to make Melanctha confess her love
for John. "In every way that he could think of in his anger he

tried to make her say a thing she did not really know" (p. 95). By refusing to speak, Melanctha wins in this struggle with her father and "began to know her power ... Melanctha now really was beginning as a woman" (p. 95).

Though she begins to know "this power" she is only dimly cognizant of its meaning and is entirely ignorant of what it is she wants. Since Melanctha feels "it was only men that held anything there was of knowledge and power," she roams through railroad yards, docks, and construction sites. The sexuality pervading these scenes is rendered in euphemistic terms:

Melanctha came here very often and watched the men and all the things that were so busy working. The men always had time for, "Hullo sis, do you want to sit on my engine," and "Hullo that's a pretty lookin' yaller girl, do you want to come and see him cookin" (p. 98).

Since "Melanctha wanted very much to know and yet feared the knowledge" (p. 101), she is attracted to these men and yet keeps her distance from them. The strategies she uses to keep this distance echo those she used in her rebellious struggle with her father. These strategies are essentially based upon a combined inability to articulate her meaning and an ability to use what "she can't say" to advantage. She lets them believe she knows something of "worldly wisdom" and escapes before they find that she doesn't:

Some man would learn a good deal about her in the talk, never altogether truly, for Melanctha all her life did not know how to tell a story wholly. She always and yet not with intention, managed to leave out big pieces which make a story very different, for when it came to what had happened and what she had said and what it was that she had really done, Melanctha never could remember right.... The man thinking that she really had world wisdom would not make his meaning clear, and believing that she was deciding with him never went so fast that he could stop her when at last she made herself escape (pp. 100-01).

If Melanctha keeps herself "safe" by not allowing meaning— her own or the man's she is attracted to—to be made clear, the narrator condemns this as cowardly. "She knew she was not getting what she so badly wanted, but with all her breakneck courage Melanctha here was a coward, and so she could not learn to really understand" (p. 97). Because she simply repeats this "cowardly" behavior with men, Melanctha wanders on "the edge of wisdom" until she discovers a different route, for it was "not from the men that Melanctha learned her wisdom" (p. 104), but from a woman, Jane Harden.

If the nature of heterosexual love can at least be suggested through euphemism, the nature of woman's power and sexuality is something that cannot even be spoken by the text. The precise nature of what Jane teaches Melanctha is not demonstrated or described; Melanctha's gradual accumulation of knowledge is simply insisted upon: "In these years Melanctha came to see very clearly what it is that gives the world its wisdom."

Melanctha's new knowledge in turn informs her relationship with Jeff. In this relationship Melanctha becomes the teacher and Jeff the student who, much like Melanctha in her relationships with men, is "cowardly," attracted to the unknown, to sexuality and to excitement but at the same time afraid of it. Thus what Melanctha has to teach him not only remains unspoken, but its very incapacity to be spoken lies at the basis of their relationship, generating endlessly repetitive dialogues frequently punctuated by their protests: "I certainly don't just see what you mean by what you say." The two of them are speaking opposing languages, which are simply played against each other. Each protests the insufficiency of the language of the other:

Melanctha: It don't seem to me Dr. Campbell that what you say and what you do seem to have much to do with each other.

Jeff: It certainly does seem to me you don't know very well yourself what you mean, when you are talking (pp. 117-18).

The text at this central point in the Melanctha story simply becomes a performance of Jeff and Melanctha's inability to communicate. The content, their "meaning," is emptied as what they say becomes less important than saying that they cannot say "it"—a much repeated indefinite pronoun. Words become excessive in two respects. They are beside the point. If Melanctha withdraws more and more into silence, explaining "it ain't much use to talk about what a woman is really feeling" (p. 135), Jeff's attempts to formulate his every thought are constantly thwarted until he finally arrives at the point where "he now never thought about all this in real words anymore" (p. 136). But words are also excessive in that they are literally multiplied in Jeff and Melanctha's effort to understand each other. This hyperbolic verbiage only serves to underline the word's emptiness, just as Jeff and Melanctha's repeated use of the words "certainly" and "surely" only serves to emphasize how they know nothing for certain: "I certainly know now really, how I don't know anything for sure at all about you Melanctha" (p. 139).

This hyperbolic language, achieved by the excruciating effort to know what can't be known and to say what can't be said, generates one of the major stylistic differences between *Q.E.D.* and its rewriting in "Melanctha." In *Q.E.D.* Adele's uncertainty about Helen's silences is protected by a much more self-righteous attitude. In an exchange between Adele and Helen, Adele poses a question that Jeff will later put to Melanctha: "Helen," she said one day, I always had an impression that you talked a great deal but apparently you are a most silent being. What is it? Do I talk so hopelessly much that you get discouraged with it as a habit?" Helen responds that she talks only with "superficial acquaintances," but is silent with friends, and that, in fact, her talk bores Adele. Impatient with this response, Adele says, "Surely one has to hit you awfully hard to shake your realler things to the surface."[19]

If Adele has the last word here, and is ready to resort to violence to extort Helen's meaning from her, Melanctha, in the rewritten exchange, feels the power of her silences and her sexuality, and Jeff is less certain about his ability to understand Melanctha:

"I certainly did think Melanctha you was a great talker from the way Jane Harden and everybody said things to me, and from the way I heard you talk so much when I first met you. Tell me true Melanctha,

why don't you talk more now to me, perhaps it is I talk so much I
don't give you any chance to say things to me...."

Melanctha smiled, with her strong sweetness, on him, and she felt
her power very deeply. "I certainly never do talk very much when I
like anybody really, Jeff. You see, Jeff, it ain't much use to talk about
what a woman is really feeling in her...."

"I don't say, no never now any more, you ain't right, Melanctha,
when you really say things to me. Perhaps I see it all to be very
different when I come to really see what you mean by what you are
always saying to me" (p. 135).

Though the vocabulary of this passage is sharply limited in
contrast to the vocabulary of *Q.E.D.*, the number of words is
multiplied. This amplification is achieved by the repetition of
qualifying words such as "really," "always," "certainly," and
the repeated use of names or insistent qualifying phrases such
as "I don't say ever," or "I certainly" or "You see" to introduce
sentences. These repeated qualifiers impede the progress of the
dialogue even as they are meant to promote it; and Stein's
repeated effort to explain May Bookstaver's enigma and silences only yields to more uncertainty. Repetition, which has
come to be associated with Stein as one of her major stylistic
devices, thus appears to have been born in the evolution of a
repeated effort to ascertain the uncertain, to speak the un-
speakable and to be at rest.

If the repeated effort of desire seeking to express itself only
yields to the longing of a hyperbolic language for silence, this
is analogous to Melanctha's major dilemma: "Melanctha Herbert was always seeking rest and quiet, and always she could
only find new ways to be in trouble" (p. 89). With slight vari-
ations, this refrain is continuously repeated, and indeed, its
dialectic structures the text. In situation after situation, Melanctha is propelled by "excitement" and desire, only to be
pulled back by her desire for rest and safety. After Melanctha
ends her relationship with the stable and methodical Jeff, who
insists upon "regular living," she turns to his complete opposite,
the playboy and gambler Jem, who insists upon taking risks.
This excitement, however, simply regenerates Melanctha's adamant insistence upon its closure through marriage. When Jem
rejects her, Melanctha sacrifices her need for excitement com-

pletely by turning to the safety of absolute submission to Rose Johnson. Melanctha becomes Rose's servant, "always very humble to her . . . Melanctha needed badly to have Rose always willing to let Melanctha cling to her. Rose was a simple, sullen, selfish black girl, but she had a solid power in her" (p. 210). Appropriately, Rose, who is simply concerned with keeping up the appearances of propriety, finally ends this relationship because of Melanctha's reputation for wandering; thus, the whole cycle is in danger of beginning again. Melanctha, however, has become increasingly debilitated by her search for a form to give her desire. Without Rose, "Melanctha was lost, and all the world went whirling in a mad weary dance around her" (p. 233). As though the power of her desire had entirely "consumed" her, Melanctha dies abruptly thereafter of consumption.

Though Melanctha's death seems abrupt, even excessive, death in fact not only pervades the story, but the impulse towards it informs the story's dynamic. Beginning and ending, life and death, are constantly conflated, as though the story were overly anxious for its own conclusion. The story for Melanctha's life begins in a situation near her death, and opens with the death of Rose's newborn baby. Jeff and Melanctha begin their relationship while tending to her dying mother. Near the end of their relationship, when Jeff is caring for a dying man, there is a highly compressed scene in which Jeff's dull "sodden" feelings are reawakened by his piercing awareness of a beautiful spring day. His renewal of joy and "sharp feeling" simultaneously brings about his hope for a new beginning with Melanctha and his knowledge that the relationship will soon end. And the repetitive refrain of "Melanctha" constantly reminds us that Melanctha seeks repose—a form of death—even as she can only find "new ways to get excited." Thus, the middle of the story—its plot—attempts to avoid the ending by the repetitive act of beginning again and again with a repetitious refrain; this refrain, however, insistently reminds us of the strain towards the story's conclusion and the character's death.

Freud ascribed the compulsion to repeat to the unconscious repressed and, ultimately, to the death instinct. He first observed that "the repressed constantly seeks to return to the present, whether in the form of dreams, symptoms, or acting out."[20] This observation became the basis for analytic treatment. The greater the resistance to the repressed material, the more extensively the patient would "act it out." Freud pointed out that by repeating an experience we become master of it; he described a child's mastery of his mother's absence by a game of throwing away and retrieving a favorite toy again and again as an example of this. However, since what was repressed was a traumatic experience, Freud later had difficulty in explaining how the compulsion to repeat was in the service of the pleasure principle. As Laplanche describes it: "Freud saw the mark of the 'daemonic' in this compulsion, the mark in other words of an irrepressible force which was independent of the pleasure principle and apt to enter into opposition with it. It was starting from this idea that Freud was brought to wonder whether instinct might not have a retrogressive character, and this hypothesis pushed to its logical conclusion, led him to see the death instinct as the very epitome of instinct. The compulsion to repeat was the essential characteristic of the death instinct: the urge to return to an earlier state and, in the last reckoning the return to the absolute repose of the inorganic."[21] Hence Freud's paradoxical conclusion in *Beyond the Pleasure Principle* that "the aim of all life is death," a conclusion that is highly analogous to the condensed juxtaposition of life and death in the Melanctha story.

All conventional narratives exploit the repetition compulsion and the desire for death.[22] The conventional structure of beginning, middle, and ending constantly replays for us our relationship to temporality; for Walter Benjamin this meant that "death is the sanction of everything that the storyteller can tell. He has borrowed his authority from death."[23] Benjamin goes on to point out that the reader's "consuming interest" in the novel is his knowledge that death awaits him at the end:

It is a dry material on which the burning interest of the reader feeds. "A man who dies at the age of thirty-five," said Moritz Heiman once, "is at every point in his life a man who dies at the age of thirty-five." Nothing is more dubious than this sentence but for the sole reason that the tense is wrong. A man—so says the truth that was meant here—who died at thirty-five will appear to remembrance at every point in his life as a man who dies at the age of thirty-five. In other words, the statement that makes no sense for real life becomes indisputable for remembered life. The nature of the character in a novel cannot be presented any better than is done in this statement, which says that the "meaning of his life" is revealed only in his death. Therefore he must, no matter what, know in advance that he will share their experience of death: if need be their figurative death—the end of the novel—but preferably their actual one. How do the characters make him understand that death is already waiting for them— a very definite death in a very definite place? That is the question which feeds the reader's consuming interest in the events of the novel.[24]

Benjamin's observation suggests that on one level, Melanctha's "excitement" which generates the movement toward a conclusion that is powerfully attractive yet necessarily destructive, a movement which in effect destroys the desire which generates it, is analogous to the process of reading, the desire for narrative.

In his excellent analysis of this narrative dynamic, Peter Brooks suggests another function of repetition in the conventional novel. Repetitive elements are a way of "binding" the narrative, of securing meaning and significance.[25] To carry this a step further, in the traditional novel, literary propriety dictates that repetition be kept discreet, that it unobtrusively establish a pattern which can only present itself to the reader through "remembrance," i.e., retrospectively. While in the process of reading, it is necessary that the reader "forget" so that the illusion of progress toward a conclusion fraught with meaning, conventionally the character's destiny or the meaning of his life, can be sustained. This is a conclusion, however, which has been actually implicit in every repeated element.

Like the reader's desire which compels her to forget and to eagerly continue to read, Melanctha's impulse toward excitement compels her to "forget" and this process is temporarily liberating. Melanctha finds her father "unendurable" but after she wins a "new power" in her fight with him, she soon "forgot to hate her father, in her strong interest in the power she now knew she had within her" (p. 95). Since a relationship of love and hate would have bound her to him, this forgetfulness liberates her for more wandering in "search of wisdom." Similarly, she "forgets" that she learned her wisdom from Jane Harden; strengthened by her forgetfulness and her new "wisdom," she becomes both stronger than Jane and bored by her, and moves on. The fact that she cannot "remember right" is not only a practical problem for Jeff since she constantly forgets her appointments with him, but also a philosophical problem since her inability to "remember right" contributes to his inability to understand her and is one of the issues upon which they part ways. Her forgetfulness, then, allows her the illusion of "mastery" but it also guarantees that she will be locked in a repetitious pattern of mastery and servitude.

Stein forces to the surface and makes excessive the implicit function of repetition in conventional narrative. In doing so, the contradictions of conventional narrative become manifest. A character who cannot remember is caught within a narrative that literally cannot forget. Moreover, these repetitive refrains insistently remind us that a character who could not express her meaning will be ultimately granted meaning only in her final repose: that the point of her story, her life, is really only her death. This is similar to Benjamin's demonstration of the paradox that the man who dies at thirty-five will appear to remembrance only as the man who died at thirty-five. The conclusion of "Melanctha" which is implicit in the repeated refrain of the story, is both perfectly logical and perfectly inadequate.

In this respect, it is significant that Melanctha's relationship with Rose both poses the story's initial enigma and guarantees the story's closure. Rose, with her "mock" yet oppressive propriety, seems to crudely epitomize all those characters in Stein's novels who were allowed to "own" May Bookstaver. Stein's dissatisfaction with these characters' repressive propriety— Mabel's in *Q.E.D.*, Miss Thornton's in *Fernhurst*, and Rose's— always instigates the telling of the story. At the same time she appropriates their power to oppress and repress as instrumental in guaranteeing the closure of the story. In the "Melanctha" story this process is highly conflated and condensed. Just as the story of Melanctha's life begins near her death and just as the story opens with the death of Rose's newborn baby, these characters bring to life a narrative which they are also responsible for putting to death. On the narrative level, this death or closure is temporary, of course, for their acts of repression—and Stein's—continually welcome the return of the repressed; and thus the story only regenerates its repetitive retelling in another of Stein's fictions.

The "Melanctha" story is Stein's strongest indication of dissatisfaction with the inability of repetitive retelling to generate new knowledge. To a certain extent Mabel was inadequate to May, Miss Thornton to Janet Bruce's "wondrous knowledge," but Rose is the most crudely inadequate of all. Not only is her "propriety," for instance, her insistence upon being "properly engaged" to each of the many men she sees, comic rationalization, but this character who is responsible for the life and death of the narrative is notably irresponsible about both life and death. Rose cannot keep her baby alive because she is too careless, but its death also leaves her nonchalant:

Rose Johnson was careless and negligent and selfish, and when Melanctha had to leave for a few days, the baby died. Rose Johnson had liked the baby well enough and perhaps she just forgot it for awhile, anyway the child was dead and Rose and Sam her husband were very sorry but these things came so often in the negro world in Bridgepoint, that they neither of them thought about it very long (p. 85).

Stein capitalizes upon the negro community's overfamiliarity with death to make a statement about Melanctha's submission to Rose, and beyond this, perhaps, the reader's submission to the framework of the conventional narrative. The conventional narrative both familiarizes us with and reconciles us to death. As Freud remarked, "fiction makes it possible for us to reconcile ourselves to death . . . we die in the person of a given hero, yet we survive him and are ready to die again with the next hero just as safely."[26] In "Melanctha," however, death has become so conventional, and at the same time so excessive, that it is meaningless. Furthermore, Melanctha's meaning, that which cannot be spoken within the framework of the conventional narrative, is lost. Although Freud speaks of a "hero," the conclusion of the traditional novel just as often, if not more frequently, left the heroine silenced or dead.

The other conventional option for the heroine at the novel's conclusion is marriage. Melanctha's desire is always so "complex" that she never manages to get herself "properly engaged" like Rose. Lena, however, is not only given the option; it becomes an option given to her with a vengeance. Unlike Melanctha, who yearns for repose but can only find new ways to get excited, Lena is simply the absolute epitome of repose. She rarely speaks, she is docile to the point of inertia, and the most frequently repeated phrase associated with her is that "she did not know." Lena has barely any consciousness at all. Instead, she is "always sort of dreamy and not there." This makes Lena, in her Aunt Mathilda's eyes, eminently suitable for a plot to marry her off.

Lena's Aunt Mathilda is the precise opposite of Miss Mathilda in "The Good Anna". While Miss Mathilda was hesitant, flabby, and incapable of exerting authority, Aunt Mathilda is "all a compact and well-hardened mass," who is "firm, directing and repressed" (p. 243). Aunt Mathilda is the sort of person who likes to advise "all of her relations how to do things better. She arranged their present and their future for them, and showed them how in the past they had been wrong in all their methods" (p. 244). No one else is allowed to hold any expectations as to their future, for Miss Mathilda is in firm possession of that category. And her expectations for Lena and her plot for Lena's future are entirely conventional: to rescue Lena from a dreary, rough life in Germany by bringing her to the new world where she will prosper first through service and then through marriage. Mathilda is granted some "wisdom," despite her "hardness," in recognizing "the rarer strain there was in Lena" (p. 245). This "rarer strain," however, is hardly important to her plot for Lena; this feature is so rare it never manages to come into existence. Mathilda is so set in her course that it does not matter that Lena really does not know that she doesn't like it in Germany, and is therefore not really in need of rescuing. Indeed, Lena's unconsciousness suits Mathilda perfectly: it guarantees the smooth running of her plot. If Miss Mathilda's secret identification with the rebels disrupted Anna's attempts to keep them in line, almost nothing prevents Aunt Mathilda from getting her way.

However, if no one rebelled or resisted, Aunt Mathilda would not have the opportunity to explain to everyone that her efforts, undertaken, after all, for their benefit, are not sufficiently appreciated. Lena is hardly capable of rebellion, but Mathilda will take the least opportunity, which ironically presents itself when Lena is being the most silent and submissive:

Why don't you answer with some sense, Lena, when I ask you if you don't like Herman Kreder. You stand there so stupid and don't answer just like you ain't heard a word what I been saying to you. I never see anybody like you, Lena. If you going to burst out at all, why don't you burst out sudden instead of standing there so silly and don't answer. And here I am so good to you, and find you a good husband so you can have a place to live in all your own (p. 252).

In this case, Mathilda must imagine that Lena is about to rebel in order to get the resistence she needs to justify her self-righteousness. Lena's fiancé, Herman Kreder, on the other hand, actually does rebel and therefore provides the only complication to the plot. Although as a young man completely submissive to his parents and lacking all desire to struggle, Herman Kreder seems perfectly suited for the role Mathilda expects him to play, just the thought of marriage is enough to bring him to life and give him the strength to resist his elders for the first time. Herman escapes to New York on the day of his wedding, leaving Lena, the innocent party, to suffer through Aunt Mathilda's scolding:

She scolded her hard because she was so foolish, and now Herman had gone off and nobody could tell where he had gone to, and all because Lena always was so dumb and silly. . . .Mrs. Hayden did not think that any old people should be good to their children. Their children always were so thankless, and never paid any attention, and older people were always doing things for their good. Did Lena think it gave Mrs. Haydon any pleasure, to work so hard to make Lena happy, and get her a good husband, and then Lena was so thankless and never did anything that anybody wanted. It was a lesson to poor Mrs. Hayden not to do things any more for anybody (p. 256).

Lena doesn't want to get married to Herman, though she is entirely willing to do so anyway, but her aunt convinces her that she should feel embarrassed that Herman ran off, and that she, somehow, is to blame. Herman, meanwhile, escapes blame entirely. His family deems it wiser to deal with him gently and to cajole him back to Lena with the enticement that "It do you good really Herman to get married and then you got somebody you can boss around when you want to" (p. 265).

With Lena and Herman married and her plot concluded to her satisfaction, Aunt Mathilda drops all her concern for Lena. Lena simply becomes more and more miserable and silent under the even sterner command of her mother-in-law. Herman, meanwhile, grows stronger through his marriage and the prospect of becoming a father. Though he was previously as inert as Lena, he begins to struggle against his mother's attitude toward Lena, not because he is worried about Lena, but because he is worried about the child she is carrying. He grows strong enough to insist that they live away from his parents and to take complete charge of their children. Each new child brings Herman more and more to life, while they make Lena more dispensable and bring her closer and closer to death. Lena dies, finally, in childbirth.

Lena's only function in the story, then, is to bring other characters to life. She herself is quite dispensable, once this task is accomplished. And the only requirements for this task are silence, submission, and lack of desire. In short, she is required not to exhibit too much life. Therefore, because Lena exerts no will, like Anna, nor has any desire, like Melanctha, she provides no resistance to the plot whatsoever, and Lena's story is the shortest of the three because she is practically dead from the beginning.

Lena is not the victim of her husband but of a conventional plot and framework. Stein simply takes a male and female of the same caliber and shows this plot to be advantageous to the male and devastating to the female. Taken to its logical conclusion, this conventional plot simply requires the woman's death. In *Three Lives*, Stein takes this conclusion and insists upon it. By doing so she offers both a devastating commentary upon women's lives in conventional frameworks and a new possibility. For her very excess of insistence, generated by repetitive retelling and manifested in repetitive refrains, breaks the linear progress of the plot and offers the possibility of a new style. That which is excessive is generally considered to be style, style being that which somehow only enhances the core of truth which is the text. But an analysis of Stein's style reveals this excess to be not only implicit in, but vital to the structure of the conventional core of "truth" in the text. Aware of the nature of repetition, and the ways in which it both relies upon repression and generates an overfamiliarity with death, Stein accomplished her first break with conventional representation by stylizing and performing this mode of representation's requirements. However, she was also to go further than this, for Stein was not content to rely upon the performance of a device which repressed the woman's voice. Instead, her later works, beginning with *The Making of Americans*, come to more closely resemble Melanctha's "silences"—her inability to remember and to "tell a story wholly." Repetition, which relies upon memory and sameness, as Stein was later to point out, was the "soothing" tranquilizer of the conventional narrative.[27] To this tranquilizer, Stein juxtaposed difference, the Will to Live, and her own later writings.

IV

Beginning and Beginning Again: The Discomposing Composition of *The Making of Americans*

Beginnings are important nay to our modern world almost more important than fulfillment. (Gertrude Stein, *The Making of Americans*)

Truth [classical] narratives tell us, is what is at the end of expectation. (Roland Barthes, *S/Z*)

I. Resolutions

This is a comforting thing in being a great author inside one that always even with much lonely feeling and much sighing in one and even with not pleasantness inside any one just then when it is a very sombre burden then that one is beginning having coming saying that pleasant living is a pleasant thing and to be explaining how some are liking pleasant living. (*The Making of Americans*)

From 1902, when she sat in the British Museum conscientiously absorbing the lessons of centuries of narrative prose, through the apprenticeship of three completed novels, through the accumulation of several notebooks filled with the ideas, observations, plot elements, and diagrams which were to inform her fourth book, Gertrude Stein bent her energy toward the accomplishment of an ambitious task: to become a "great author." The project which was to stand as testimony to this accomplishment, a project which she began again and again and finally completed in 1911, was *The Making of Americans*. Stein considered this book to be one of her most important achievements, worthy of taking its stand as one of the three great books of the century, a book that "everyone ought to be reading."[1] My purpose here is not to judge what could be considered extravagant claims for both herself and her book, but to discuss the evolution of her effort to justify these claims, an evolution amply recorded in *The Making of Americans*. Stein's intentions for her project, as a multitude of programmatic statements within the novel reveal, were developed "gradually" and became ever more expansive over the course of the eight years of its composition. She began with the simple intention to tell the history of a single American family, then broadened her focus to include "the progress" of three generations of two American families, and finally evolved the task of telling the "history of everyone who is or has been living." But in the course of the book's own "progress" each of her aims and intentions became subsumed and transformed by a larger objective. For by preserving intact each of its many new beginnings, projected aims, and stylistic experiments, this mammoth book is finally the record of Stein's first sustained struggle and self-conscious confrontation with the act of composition itself, of what it means to author and to be an "author."

The framework of her story—the family history of three generations—was a conventionally appropriate one in which to confront and conceptualize authorship. Both the act of procreation and the struggle between generations have always been common metaphors in Western culture for imagining the author's own act of begetting, generating, or creating something new, an issue that would both acknowledge and appropriate parental authority. The novel, in particular, acquires its authority by reference to familial origins, both in its subject matter and form. The novel not only uses the middle-class family and its history as a breeding ground for further adventures, and the struggle with parental authority as a central complication, but the "narrative's teleology, that is, narrative purpose, tendency, and endpoint, shapes and is shaped by a life story, a father begetting and generating, a mother giving birth, a child marrying and begetting or dying or both."[2] Genealogy and generation, then, provide the novel with a sense of time which is sequential, causal, chronological. As Edward Said puts it:

Narrative's chief aim is to wed inaugural promise to time—to be in other words, the course of such a marriage, the issue of which is discovery, explanation, genealogy. The narrative represents the generative process—literally in its mimetic representation of men and women in time, metaphorically in that by itself it generates succession and multiplication of events after the manner of human procreation.[3]

By proposing to render the "history" of a family who emigrated from the old world to the new, and the "progress" of their attempts over three generations to both assimilate and advance, then, Stein began to confront her own act of authority by planting herself solidly within the novel's most familiar and solid territory.

Said, however, makes it clear that the guarantor of the novel's "inaugural promise" is not the matriarch of the family, but its patriarch: "the novel's beginning premise is paternal."[4] It is the father's generative power, his authority, that are at stake in the novel; as Roland Barthes points out, both narrative conflict and pleasure are oedipal:

The death of the Father would deprive literature of many of its pleasures. If there is no longer a Father, why tell stories? Doesn't every narrative lead back to Oedipus? Isn't story-telling always a way of searching for one's origins, speaking one's conflict with the law, entering into the dialectic of tenderness and hatred? ... As fiction Oedipus was at least good for something: to make good novels, to tell good stories.[5]

The passage from ignorance to knowledge, the familiar trajectory of the realistic novel, re-enacts the oedipal drama; the resolution speaks to one's reconciliation with the father's truth, with the "way things are" in patriarchal culture. Within this self-enclosed self-perpetuating cycle, a circle constantly re-drawn, only the son can legitimately take the father's place.

> The novel moves from the naive, mystified position of the son, who understands and sees nothing, to the position of knowledge of the father who has gone through a similar experience and has supposedly transcended (understood) the conflict between generations and its truth (Oedipus).[6]

Thus the novel becomes a ritualistic quest for, and confirmation of, male, patriarchal authority.

With her gender excluded from authority by this repetitive cycle, the woman who would write must first contend with what Sandra Gilbert and Susan Gubar have demonstrated to be a debilitating "anxiety of authorship."[7] As we have seen, Stein's strategy for dealing with this anxiety was to assert her "male-ness," to resolutely deny that she was "born a woman." This strategy has the paradoxical effect of both accepting and de-nying culturally produced categories and definitions as natural truths. In effect, Stein was creating a position for herself as an anomaly. Yet, although she felt herself to be "singular" and anomalous, her attempts to deny this paradox were always stronger than her acknowledgment of it. Thus she began her own quest to be an author by accepting patriarchal authority as universal truth and resolutely attempting to appropriate it. Her first gesture toward writing *The Making of Americans* speaks both to this resolution and her dissatisfaction with it.

Stein wrote this small fragment early in 1903; thus, her ambition to write her great American novel predates the com-position of *Q.E.D.*[8] When Stein began her novel again in 1906, she expanded upon this fragment, broadened her focus, and changed her emphasis. In the 1903 fragment, however, she limits her story to one German Jewish immigrant family, the Dehnings, who have assimilated themselves into a comfortably Anglo-Saxon middle-class life style. In the opening paragraph she announces that her intention is to explain the creation of American character: "The old people in a new world, the new people made out of the old"; and she places all her faith in the novel's familiar home, the middle-class family, as capable of

producing "the best the world can know."[9] But her celebratory
intention is complicated by her more pressing narrative concern to explain the disastrous marriages of the two Dehning
daughters, Julia and Bertha. Her explanation for these marriages involves her in a direct contradiction: the middle-class
family is criticized as being incapable of appreciating or even
recognizing true "singularity." Instead of vindicating conventional middle-class wisdom she questions it, and instead of
generating a happy ending her celebration ends first in resignation, and then in the irresolute attempt to begin again.

Stein's battle with her contradictory impulses is played out
in a weak battle with the conventional novel's creation of character. Julia Dehning seems to offer the possibility for a strong
new beginning. She is a headstrong, ambitious, and passionately idealistic spokeswoman for modern ideas; and, advocating
new ideas herself, the narrator warns us that her creation of
Julia will not fulfill our expectations formulated by "storybook
traditions." However, Julia's limitations seem to speak to the
narrator's own fears in this regard. For Julia's passionate aspirations are limited by her "spare American imagination"
which can only shape her desire in the "form of moral idealism."
Julia is attracted to Henry Hersland because he seems to offer
"culture" with a "strain of romance" but in truth he is not
really "singular." The American bourgeois mind, the narrator
tells us, is attracted to "a singularity that yet keeps within the
limits of conventional respectability, a singularity that is so to
speak well-dressed and well set up."[10] Similarly, the narrator
ultimately allows her own attraction to singularity to speak
within the confines of a completely conventional plot. For Julia's destiny is ultimately explained and shaped by her struggle
with her father over their differing concepts of her fiancé. This
struggle generates a conventional dramatic sequence aiming
at discovery and marriage: the heroine progresses from her
youthful and passionately held illusions through struggle to a
disillusioned but wiser maturity.

Julia's father—whose appropriately patriarchal name is
Abraham—distrusts Hersland immediately, not because Hers-
land is not truly "singular" but because he seems unreliable.
Abraham does not make his judgment on the basis of any con-

crete evidence; he is simply granted the power of seeing through appearances and knowing the truth. "He comes of a family that are all successful and well-appearing," Abraham tells Julia, "and I say I don't know anything against him but I don't quite trust him."[11] Though his children admire and respect their father, who is wise, tolerant, and capable of making sharp judgments, they must nevertheless argue with him because "he was the old generation, they the new and with all his wisdom surely he must fail to see the meaning in the unaccustomed."[12] Therefore Julia debates with her father, feeling that his "keen completed look that was so full of its own understanding" left "no room in it for any other kind of meaning."[13] By steadfast argument, Julia gains a brief victory and wins her father's permission to marry Hersland.

However, Julia can not ultimately win, for the narrator herself has sacrificed her own concern for "singularity" and the "unaccustomed" by conceding to and appropriating the wisdom of the father. In the biblical story, when Isaac trusts and submits to the will of his father, Abraham, who in turn trusts and submits to the will of God, he is redeemed and his faith rewarded. By ultimately submitting and trusting to the mechanisms of the conventional patriarchal plot, the narrator must sacrifice Julia. Julia begins to discover her "mistake" and her father's wisdom when Hersland begins to hint that he wants his father-in-law's backing to gamble on questionable schemes. Julia has a brief moment of insight, when she sees her father's reality—"things as they were and not as she had wished them"— but the momentum of her idealistic illusions carry her forward into what the narrator considers will be a miserable marriage. Similarly, the narrator resolves the novel's conflicts and her doubts too quickly and, in her ultimate acceptance and appropriation of patriarchal authority, rushes too rapidly toward an inevitable conclusion.

This "realistic" portrait of Julia, then, simply confirms the woman's oppressed place in the patriarchal order, an order wherein, as the narrator notes, men have "all the simple rights in a sane and simple world,"[14] and where the woman's truth is to be repressed, or acknowledged as an "illusion" or mistake. Julia defines herself solely against her father's values by her struggle with him. Her struggle with her mother, on the other hand, simply consists of a struggle to repress her: "... a large part of our family history," the narrator tells us, "must be a record of her struggle to live down her mother in her."[15] Julia's "new beginning"—her marriage—and the narrator's attempt to escape "storybook traditions" end by simply validating the father's privileged position as the repository of wisdom. Abraham combines both the function of *pater familias*, who can theoretically be superseded, and God the father, who sees and knows all and cannot be superseded. The father, in other words, is at first implicated in, but ultimately transcends, the struggle between generations. Since the father is a transcendent standard, and thus the measure for all departures, this short fragment posits not a new beginning but a divine origin.

Where to begin to speak but within the patriarchal framework? Julia's ideals and consequently her mistaken choice, the narrator explains at one point, arose from her naive belief that all men were "honoring and honorable." But given the nature of her world and upbringing, this naive belief was the only one available to her. For Julia to doubt, to believe otherwise, would be "to imagine a vain thing, to recreate her world and make a new one all from her own head."[16] If Stein's narrator acknowledges the difficulty of creating a new world, of speaking otherwise, she nonetheless does make an irresolute attempt in this short fragment to do so. In the attempt to halt narrative momentum, the narrator digresses, often to urge her readers to "arm yourselves with patience" and not to hold conventional expectations. These digressions, however, are quickly suppressed. In a sentence which clearly reveals this dynamic, the narrator says: "However let us take comfort, beginnings are important nay to our modern world almost more important than fulfillment and so we go cheerily on with our story."[17] The temptation to doubt the aim of the story—fulfillment—is quickly suppressed by the desire to "cheerily" carry on, to breed continuity and plot, a desire which soon builds into the implacable momentum to fulfill expectation. In the last few pages of the fragment, the narrator attempts to begin again by formulating Julia's character in a different way, a way that would escape the dramatic momentum of the realistic novel by simply setting up contrasts. Julia, who had "rushed upon her sorrow [her marriage] passionately, fervently, heroically," is compared to her sister Bertha, who "sank down into hers [her marriage] quietly, helplessly, unaspiringly."[18] Stein's contrast of opposing types, here, is a forerunner of her attempt to classify "kinds of people" in *The Making of Americans*. However, the fragment picks up the narrative line again before this alternative is really explored, and the story finally comes to an abrupt halt in the middle of a sentence.

Stein seemed incapable of imagining not only a "happy ending" but even a "character" for women in terms of the options within a patriarchal framework. Yet, in her next three novels, her quarrel with patriarchal resolutions and formulations of character re-enact the same dynamic tension revealed in her first gesture toward writing *The Making of Americans*. Disruptive doubts are too quickly resolved and the need to express a woman's desire is too quickly repressed in the rush to complete the story and to appropriate patriarchal authority and power. As long as Stein continued to both rebel against this authority, and to appropriate it by identification and repression, the cycle is perpetually repeated. It is only in "Melanctha," where the repeated insistence upon a woman's doubt and sexuality is repeatedly met, of course, by an equally adamant repression, where, in other words, the cycle's tensions are extremely conflated and excessively repeated that the story line becomes radically disrupted and subverted. For, in stylizing this cycle by excessively repeating it, Stein turns the story into a performance of its own generative tension, and the story line's conventional generative impulse of succession and continuity is actively disrupted just as the momentum toward its inevitable conclusion is both insisted upon and delayed. *Three Lives* makes it explicit that the progression toward the conclusion in the conventional novel is the inevitable pull toward death—or a form of death (inertia, resignation to "things as they are" or the status quo) itself. Thus the executors of her narrative, those representatives of patriarchal authority responsible for the story's conclusion, progressively, and more insistently and explicitly play out the murderous impulse behind patriarchal authority implicit in Stein's reference to the biblical story of Abraham in the 1903 fragment.

A major paradox behind patriarchal authority, as Susan Gubar and Sandra Gilbert point out, is that the author silences and imprisons his characters even as he gives them life, "silences...stills them...and kills them."[19] In *The Making of Americans* Stein meditates upon this paradox in a parable about a father and son:

One of such of these kind of them had a little boy and this one, the little son wanted to make a collection of butterflies and beetles and it was all exciting to him and it was all arranged then and then the father said to the son you are certain this is not a cruel thing that you are wanting to be doing, killing things to make collections of them, and the son was very disturbed then and they talked about it together the two of them and more and more they talked about it then and then at last the boy was convinced it was a cruel thing and he said he would not do it and his father said the little boy was a noble boy to give up pleasure when it was a cruel one. The boy went to bed then and then the father when he got up in the early morning saw a wonderfully beautiful moth in the room and he caught him and he killed him and he pinned him and he woke up his son then and showed it to him and he said to him see what a good father I am to have caught and killed this one, the boy was all mixed up inside him and then he said he would go on with his collecting and that was all there was then of discussing and this is a little description of something that happened once and it is very interesting.[20]

Power is entrenched, as Foucault points out, not simply because it says no, but because it provides pleasure and produces meaning.[21] In Stein's parable, the father is caught in the dilemma of saying "no" to a "cruel pleasure" and yet, perpetuating this cruel pleasure in the desire to be a "good father." In her struggle to write *The Making of Americans*, Stein became, as she later put it, "consciously obsessed" with the problem presented in her parable. Her struggle with this dilemma is a struggle to forsake the contradictory and "cruel pleasure" of killing life in order to preserve it, and to create instead a new aesthetic which would create character in a more mobile, vital, and fluid way.

The Making of Americans is the record of this struggle, however, rather than the presentation of a final or ultimate solution. Instead of defining her aesthetic in terms of a resolute appropriation of power, she defines it instead within the resolute attempt to live in irresolution itself.

II. *Beginning Again:* Red eyes, bright hankies, crazy writing

Life is strife. (Gertrude Stein, *The Mother of us All*)

We undertake to overthrow your undertaking. (Gertrude Stein, *The Mother of us All*)

If her first fragmentary gesture toward writing *The Making of Americans*, and her first three completed novels had seemed to yield to an implacable momentum toward the conclusion, a conclusion contingent upon death and the interdiction of desire, a conclusion that left those standing in the place of the father in a final position of authority, ownership, and control, her new attempt when she took up her novel again in 1906 was to delay this momentum toward the conclusion by beginning again and again. The length of the book itself is testimony to this effort; but within its generous 925 pages the quest is not for patriarchal authority but for survival itself. What gives people the will to live? In her other writings, Stein always associated this question with her favorite teacher, William James, who had lectured upon the subject.[22] In this lecture James had posited the "Will to Live" upon the will to believe, upon the establishment of meaning which would present a "live hypothesis" to us.[23] In *The Making of Americans*, Stein searches for this "live hypothesis," for her own certainty, even as she explores "everyone" else's. "Certainly," she tells us, "very many are needing that everything being living is having meaning" (p. 782), and her book is the exploration of all the possible ramifications of this statement. The threat of inherent meaninglessness is omnipresent, and in the face of this threat, how do people protect themselves? How does one attain certainty? What beliefs do people hold that allow them, not only to act with authority, but to simply "go on"? How do they establish their "sense of importance" in the face of their cosmic insignificance? The fact that these were not particularly new questions did not mean that they were posed with less passion and intensity; to the contrary, it is under the impetus of Stein's passionate quest for meaning and certainty that the question becomes so explicit and insistent.

If the intensity of her quest was to take her far beyond the parsimonious solutions of the traditional novel, "family living" as she called it, seemed to provide the most obvious starting point, an acceptable "live hypothesis." The middle-class family has produced and structured meaning in ways that have become entrenched by centuries of repetition. Its comfort as an explanatory framework is obvious: one's own insignificance can be enfolded into the roll of generations, one's identity "explained" by genealogy; and it justifies as well the need for "going on" in the need to perpetuate one's own kind. Even on the level of quotidian existence, it provides patterns for basic routine survival: it is within the context of "family living" that Stein first centers her explanation for the way "everyone eats and drinks and loves and sleeps and talks and walks and wakes and forgets and quarrels and likes and dislikes and works and sits."[24] Stein wanted to say that this existence is "vital," but what she demonstrates more convincingly, no more so than in the style she develops to render it, is its tenaciousness and monotony. Family living, as she rendered it, was finally more habitual than vital, a kind of death-in-life secured by adherence to un-thought-out premises. For one who regarded herself as "singular," who objected to being "ground in the same mill as all the others,"[25] this schema could only be, at best, an ambivalent comfort.

The epigraph to *The Making of Americans* speaks to her conflicting interest in both "singularity" and generational struggle. The epigraph is a paraphrase of a story Stein found in Aristotle's *Nichomacean Ethics* and is meant to illustrate, as Richard Bridgman has pointed out, "that men will accept 'natural' behavior more easily than they do the unorthodox."[26] The example of "natural" behavior that Aristotle gives is a story about filial anger and aggression. Stein tells it in the following way: "Once an angry man dragged his father along the ground through his own orchard. 'Stop!' cried the groaning old man at last. 'Stop!' I did not drag my father beyond this tree" (p.3).This paraphrase would seem to set up a proposal to shape and investigate character through the struggle between generations. Yet, instead of commenting on this struggle, she comments instead upon the larger issue which Aristotle is addressing: unorthodox behavior. As Bridgman notes, her comments alter Aristotle's meaning. Instead of saying that filial aggression is easier to countenance than unorthodox behavior, she expresses a tolerance for "our sins," a tolerance perhaps based upon a newly found acceptance of her own "singularity." As we get older, she says, we realize that these sins are "harmless," that they even "give charm to our character and so our struggle with them dies away" (p. 3). What Stein did not seem to realize was how far this newly found tolerance was to carry her from her literary father Aristotle and his dictates of propriety. Ideas she had formerly repressed out of a sense of conventional propriety are tolerantly considered, and so shape her book in a new way.

As we have seen, one of the people Stein felt did not belong in the story of generational struggle was the mother. But if Julia Dehning's history was to be one of "living down the mother inside her," Stein's new attempt is to somehow come to terms with the mother. In her new beginning of 1906, Stein broadens her narrative to take into account not only the Dehnings but the Herslands, a family clearly modelled upon her own. She also broadens the scope of her story to include three generations instead of two, and so more clearly focuses her story upon generational struggle. However, she opens the narrative not with the patriarchs of the two families but with the matriarchs. She characterizes these matriarchs as all "strong to bear children"; one is strong to lead her children, the others are "strong to suffer" with them.

The story of Martha Hersland, the matriarch who was "strong to lead her children," is one of the most vivid stories in *The Making of Americans*. Martha is described as "a great mountain," who has the strength "to uphold around her, her man, her family and everybody else whom she saw needed directing" (p. 36). Martha convinces her husband that it would be best for the children if the family moved to America, and with steady patience and repeated encouragements she keeps her more reluctant husband going toward that goal. "It was hard to start him and it was almost harder to keep him going" (p. 38). Mr. Hersland agrees that the move would be best for the family, but he is reluctant to "begin again" because he derives a comfortable sense of self-importance from his religion, his trade, his status in the village, in short, from the way things are. As long as his sense of self-importance is maintained by the esteem the family gains for their adventurous decision to move, by the busy activity of selling their possessions or by the small celebration of their departure, he remains confident of the plan. But when he is actually about to lose those things which guaranteed his security and importance, he tries to regain them. When it is time to actually part with the household possessions he has sold, he tries to hide them; when he sees a new butcher take his place, he wants to buy back the shop. And when the family sets out on the journey toward the ship which will carry them to America, the journey must be halted again and again for Martha to go back and find her husband who constantly returns to a point where he can view the village for "one last time" in order not to forget it. When Mr. Hersland can no longer return to a point where he can see the village, he forgets his struggle. The family is successful enough in their transition to the new world; they are mildly prosperous and Mr. Hersland is soon "content."

Just as the narrator's tone is gently ironic, Martha's power to lead is paradoxically based upon her ability to exploit a secondary, supportive role. Martha accepts her husband's conservative impulses as necessary and right, and tells him that she only wants to do what he thinks is best. Meanwhile, she ultimately wins the struggle for a new beginning for the family by gently reassuring him that he has made an important decision for the family, and that he is needed to take care of them, to "do their talking" in the new world. Because it is Martha who has made the decision to move and who seems a more convincing talker, this placating is ironic. But so too is the narrator's echo of biblical language and subject matter, an echo perhaps meant to contrast directly to the allusion to the story of Abraham in the 1903 fragment. Mr. Hersland is not the strong patriarch with a clear vision who leads his people into the new land, but rather a weak man who has a stronger stake in the past than in the future and who can only be kept in movement by a strong matriarch. The story suggests that the privileges men enjoy in a patriarchal culture—the way in which possessions, status, and religion reinforce their sense of self-importance—gives them a stronger stake in the past. Thus, the strong matriarch, who has less of a stake in this system, has the function of introducing the new.

This story is of paradigmatic significance, both in terms of its creation of an inspirational model (Stein was later to identify herself with Susan B. Anthony as "The Mother of Us All") and its language and technique. Stein does not use language to render her story in a simply descriptive or expository way, but in order to create the rhythm of movement and struggle itself. This rhythm is established by her use of repetition, which conveys not only the difficulty of overcoming Mr. Hersland's reluctance, but what this reluctance was based upon as well: the ease with which one can slip back to the stasis of comfortable positions. Repetition in this story, however, serves a double function—both to acknowledge the importance of the past and to introduce the new. Mr. Hersland's repetitive returns halt the progress of the journey, while Mrs. Hersland's repeated encouragements keep the journey going. While Mrs. Hersland does not initially convince Mr. Hersland, eventually her repeated assertions become comforting and the only "anchor" that makes a strange world seem familiar. Repetition, in other words, is not bound by inertia in this story, but released in the service of a new beginning. In *The Making of Americans*, Stein's stylistic strategy seems to evolve from her concern both to understand change and to give birth to it.

In this respect, Stein's repetitious phrases help her to hold on to an idea, an idea which she is initially unable or unwilling to explore in its full ramifications. Repeated phrases help her, as did Mr. Hersland's repeated returns, to review the starting point. In a sense, this movement speaks to her struggle with narrative momentum. For she wanted to produce a book with

narrative flow, yet she always seemed to find the linear flow
of plot development too constricting.

In the first section of the book she begins with the Dehning
family and the story of Julia's engagement and marriage to
Alfred Hersland, but she is much more interested in the three
generations of the Hersland family than in the Dehnings. She
therefore drops all concern for the Dehnings for the next three
hundred pages, but the Herslands' story seems to be a digression,
since she has already interested her reader in what happens
to Julia and Alfred. Foreseeing this, her narrator digresses in
order to justify her digression on the Herslands in a series of
oxymoronic statements that reveal her conflicting wish to both
get on with the development of her story and to take her time
in order to include everything of importance. Therefore, the
narrator tells the reader that he should be both "patient" and
"eager" because she is "slowly hastening" with her story about
the history of the middle class which is both "vital" and
"monotonous" (p. 34). And, when she is telling the story of the
Herslands, she gets sidetracked by her mother's family. The
narrative seems to waver back and forth between David
Hersland and his wife Fanny, while Stein also attempts to
introduce her generation and their life in "Gossols," a fictive
name for her childhood home in Oakland, California.

These many digressions necessitate many repetitive
statements, and many repeated "to begin agains" where, after
a long digression, some significant phrase of one narrative is
taken up and repeated and that particular story expanded. As
she begins to tell the story of the second generation (again and
again) it becomes clear the extent to which this technical
difficulty is an emotional one. For the second generation, Stein's
parents, are less inspiring and more difficult to come to terms
with than her paternal grandparents. Whereas the story of the
first-generation Herslands flowed smoothly, without digression,
the story of the second generation is hesitant, often because
Stein does not seem to quite know what to make of their lives.

Significantly, this is more the case with her mother than
with her father. Martha Hersland's son, David, who represents
Stein's father, inherits his mother's "abundance" of spirit, her
ability to be "always powerful in starting" and her pioneering

instinct, which carries him out west—the "newest part of the new world" (p. 43). Unfortunately, David does not inherit his mother's "steadfast patience" and his eccentricities and ever-changing ideas both annoy and embarrass his children. Nevertheless, as patriarch and family authority, David, we are repeatedly told, "always had the important feeling to himself inside him" and demands his children's obedience and grudging respect. The children "turned to the father, altogether in their thinking. It was against him inside . . . that they had to do the fighting for their freedom" (p. 45).

By contrast, Stein finds it more difficult to carve out an identity for her mother, who is much less definitive: "There was not any difference for her between herself and everything existing" and she is "lost in between the father and the three big resentful children" (p. 45). Her mother, in short, does not have any "importance to herself inside her that comes with the individual being" (p. 57). Yet the narrator's ability to establish one's individuality has been presented as the key to the development of her history. Her history, she tells us, is "the story of how they came each one to have their kind of important individual feeling inside them" (p. 67). Stein tenaciously attempts to resolve this dilemma by trying to tell us her mother's story, but it is a story filled with many digressions, hesitations, contradictions, and false starts. Her mother's lack of identity, in other words, challenges her methodology even as she attempts to compensate for the father and children's lack of respect and attention.

The narrator first attempts to establish Fanny's identity by means of Fanny's genealogy. First we are told that Fanny's father caused much sorrow in his family by his "importance in religion." Fanny's mother's most outstanding characteristic is her "trickling kind of weeping" (p. 44). This information is somewhat contradicted later when the narrator seems intent upon emphasizing that the father was in fact very tolerant and that Fanny's family mostly lived in mildness and contentment. The narrator cannot decide whether the family was or was not "important to themselves in their feeling," and the genealogical search to give shape to Fanny's individuality breaks down. In fact, it is not until Fanny leaves her family and moves out west with her husband that she becomes more definitive. Here, her former lifestyle—well-to-do middle-class living—gives her a modicum of distinction, separating her from the poorer people in Gossols and giving her "dignity of position." And it is in Gossols that she meets the Schilling family who "gave her her first important feeling" (p. 56).

However, after making this statement the narrator delays and digresses for many pages before she gives us the story of the Schillings. The reason for this delay becomes obvious when we meet these people for they are even more difficult than Fanny to individualize. Mrs. Schilling is like "many millions of women" who "have been chosen by a man to content him" and who are simply wives and mothers, spending their whole life "working, cooking, and directing" (p. 78). These women usually have "doughy empty heads," are so heavy they have no lap when they sit, and breathe heavily as they waddle around. Mrs. Schilling has one fat daughter and one thin one who are just about as equally unspectacular. Nevertheless, the narrator decides that it is, in fact, because they "didn't have any meaning inside them" that they are unique and important to Fanny. Their lack of meaning puzzles Fanny, and the uncertainty it causes jolts her from the ease with which she is accustomed to making judgments. One begins to feel, however, that the Schillings are more interesting in this respect to the narrator than they are to the mother. For the introduction of the Schillings gives the narrator a new interest and the narrative a new direction. This new interest is in the problem the Schillings pose, i.e., how each individual is unique and yet can be classified as a type. As far as the Schillings are concerned, the narrator finds that their only uniqueness, their "queerness," is that they are "like so many millions of others" (p. 81). Without further comment upon this paradox, the narrator soon begins to add the baggage of classifying people to her search for what gives Fanny Hersland her "first important feeling."

The narrator presents women's status in middle-class, nineteenth-century America—their very lack of identity—as both an interesting enigma and as their only useful, though not always successful weapon in a struggle for power. Martha Hersland, David's sister, for example, is successful in her struggle to direct his life by becoming "a part" of him. She succeeds in arranging David's marriage to Fanny by manipulating him through "brilliant seductive managing" (p. 87), which includes pleasing him by coaxing, flattering, and teasing. Martha Hersland, then, like her mother who goaded her husband into moving to America, leads by being supportive. The second-generation Martha's victory—the marriage—is important, the narrator tells us, because the American literary tradition does not emphasize enough those people, primarily women, who recognize the importance of simply keeping the world going. The other group of women Stein is interested in, however, are even more obscure—those who "never had any importance for anyone around them." These women, like her own mother, and like the "mother of Anna, Bertha, and Cora" have no history, "nothing to connect her to a past, present, or future" (p. 100). Furthermore, these women do not seem capable of exerting power, a crucial step in asserting one's individuality, as far as Stein is concerned. Fanny Hersland's husband always regards the "power she had in her sometimes over him as not important to him, that was only a joke to him" (p. 124). "Often" the narrator repeats again and again, "she was not even existing to him." This being the case, the narrator decides that Fanny only came to have an important feeling inside her through her relationship to those who depend upon her, the servants and governesses, particularly Madeline Wyman.

Once again, Stein long delays the story of Madeline's relationship to Fanny, this time to introduce her concept of "bottom nature." A person's bottom nature can be known by his or her repetitious behavior. Again, women seem more incoherent to her in this respect than men:

Many women have not in their middle being so much in their way of being to make it all inside them mix into a whole as most men have it in them in their middle living, they have less in the conditions of their living to make the natures in them mix together with the bottom nature of them to make a whole of them than most men have it then in them. (p. 141)

That men are more successful at "being whole" is not surprising, since women seem to be given only one option in the society Stein depicts: existing as extensions of those around them. Using David Hersland as her prime example, the narrator explains that only men could be "outside him"—women, including both his sister Martha and his wife Fanny, must all be a "part of him." Therefore, Stein initially develops her idea of "bottom nature" by talking about men, particularly her father.

When she comes to women, on the other hand, she can only define them as "kinds of people." As with the Schillings, this has the paradoxical effect of making them unique because they are like so many others:

The kinds of feeling women have in them and the ways it comes out from them makes for them the bottom nature in them, gives to them their kind of thinking, makes the character they have all their living in them, makes them their kind of women and there are always many millions made of each kind of them (p. 164).

Because women are more paradoxical to her than men, it makes sense that she should use oxymorons as a basis for her categories of "kinds of women." Women are either "independent dependent" or "dependent independent." Later she will add the categories "resisting attacking" or "attacking resisting." It is difficult, if not impossible, to sort out exactly what Stein means by these categories, though they obviously arise from her previously implicit interest in the way women assert power. These categories give her a new way to perceive her mother, who is "dependent independent" and "resisting attacking."

Stein eventually attempts to classify men according to these categories as well, but her examples are essentially taken from women's lives, and she uses these categories to describe their relationships with each other. "It is the same in men as in women," she explains at one point, "but it separates a little clearer in women and so it will make a kind of diagram for a beginning" (p. 225). Her method for this new "beginning," however odd, has the effect of giving recognition to an otherwise obscure realm of very ordinary women—servants, governesses, and mothers, daughters, and sisters from the families in Gossols—to whom nothing "dramatic" happens. With a kind of scientific detachment, the narrator surveys the "existences" of several women, a survey intended to expand, refine, and exemplify her way of knowing people. The kind of "existences" she enumerates—stupid being, anxious being, childish natures, instrumental natures—are not meant to be derogatory, but are simply presented as "interesting." "Everyone is right in their own living" (p. 464), she proclaims in a democratic spirit.

The realm of family life in Gossols implicates Fanny and her children, who are capable of being changed by it, more than it does the self-contained David. Although Fanny feels in a different position from the families in Gossols, and is in a different position, obviously, from her servants and governesses, they are responsible for her "first important feeling of herself." And the children, the narrator tells us, increasingly become a part of the poorer families in Gossols. David, on the other hand, plays a paternal, advisory, and eccentric role in the town. And he is only interested in the governesses to the extent that they suit his ever-changing and always elaborate theories of education. "Theoretically," the narrator tells us, the governess Madeline Wyman "was important to him, really she had no existence for him" (p. 239).

It is not until the final pages of the first section, when she tells the story of Fanny's relationship with Madeline Wyman, that the narrator ends her struggle to define Fanny's "sense of importance to herself." She obviously does not derive this feeling from her husband or children. When she dies, "they all soon forgot that she had ever been important to them as a wife, a mother, a mistress living among them" (p. 134). Madeline Wyman, on the other hand, was the only one who "never forgot her." Madeline grants Fanny recognition by listening to her. Their history, the narrator tells us, is "a history of their talking to each other and a history of how they owned each other" (p. 253). The threat of loss as an important awakening is one of Stein's recurring themes in *The Making of Americans*. Fanny was cut off from her "early living" in the East, and it is this loss that begins to define her. It is her need to remember this part of her life by telling about it that begins to shape her relationship to Madeline. When Madeline's parents arrange a marriage for her, Fanny fights to have Madeline stay on as her children's governess. The threat of losing her "possession"—

both her self-possession and the person who guaranteed it—prompts her first assertive act.

But the children, too, are threatened by loss—the loss of their mother to Madeline. Though they previously took their mother for granted and ignored her, they become jealous and resentful of Madeline's close relationship to Fanny. It was "an owning their mother's early living ... owning their mother's moment of being most herself to herself in her feeling ... that they felt something cut off from them. A part that should have been them Madeline Wyman held in possession" (p. 255). Because she is equally sympathetic with both the children and the mother, the narrator oscillates between asserting and denying Madeline's importance to Fanny. Finally, she decides that their relationship provided Fanny with an "important feeling" but not with her "real being." Fanny is still presented as lacking self-consciousness; she herself is not as aware as the narrator is how unimportant she is to her husband and children, or even how important Madeline is to her. The narrator, however, cannot be said to have provided us with any more of a coherent sense of Fanny's "real being" than Fanny herself possessed. What is important, however, is that her attempt to repossess the mother has provided the first section's shape and movement. Instead of automatically delegating the mother to a repressed and ignored position, the narrator again and again attempts to define her, which is set up as a part of a larger project of defining herself. Along the way, she has recognized, or "listened to," and at the same time, given voice to numerous other women who were "not important to anybody else around them." It is this democratic attempt that informs the discontinuous, contradictory experimentation of the "beginning" of *The Making of Americans*. As though she has finally arrived at a point where she can get down to business, the narrator promises to tell the story of Martha Hersland of the third generation and ends her first section with the portentous statement "to begin again" (p. 285).

However, the narrator does not deliver this story immediately, as promised. Instead, she opens the "Martha Hersland" section with the sentence: "I write for myself and strangers" (p. 289). The following two sections of *The Making of Americans* are primarily devoted to the composition of this "I," to its authority and history. And what the narrator feels is at the very basis of her authority, as she tells us, is "that always I am looking and comparing and classifying" (p. 289). In other words, her ordered system for knowing everybody is what she "loves" and what she can write about. The "I" derives its identity and authority, then, from this system, just as the narrator uses this system in order to give shape to everybody else's identity. The narrator's preoccupation with telling us about her system provides the main narrative line, and the individual histories of the Hersland children become digressions. The narrative is turned inside out and becomes the story of its speaker in the attempt to speak.

This speaker is clearly an autobiographical projection of Stein, indeed many critics assume that this "I" is no longer a narrator, but simply Stein herself making full and transparent statements. This seems plausible, for Stein herself seems to assume this transparency; there is no attempt to rhetorically distance herself from this "I" by irony or self-conscious posing. However, this assumption must be qualified. Undoubtedly, this "I" is a product of Stein's particular historical situation. Yet, this "I" is also a creation of language: "what someone says impersonates him, turns the speaker into a person and makes the writer the creation of his writing."[27] To miss the way in which the literary "voice is a function not of persons (of a 'pre-existent people creating language') but of language, of the linguistic codes and conventions that make it possible for an 'I' to appear,"[28] is to miss an important struggle in *The Making of Americans*. This "I" most often interrupts the story in order to voice problems of composition, indeed often to disclose her unhappiness with "my writing." The "I" is more often discomposed than composed by the very process meant to create it. While on the one hand, nothing is more important to Stein than the creation of this person, this "I," her constant discomposure reveals her discontent with the way in which language is creating her. This paradoxical struggle has as its outcome a critique of the very linguistic codes and conventions that make it possible for an "I" to appear.

The Making of Americans, in other words, is Stein's first

explicit attempt to come to terms with the question of identity, a question that was to haunt her for the rest of her career, and that was to have important ramifications for her changing notions of authority. In this respect, the opening of the "Martha Hersland" section, in which the writer's "I" announces her intentions, program, and problems is not as abruptly discontinuous with the first section as it first appears to be. The first section closes with Stein's attempt to give Fanny Hersland an "I" and her "sense of importance to herself." She does this, in effect, by making her an author; Fanny establishes her importance by telling Madeline Wyman her story. But Fanny's authorship and identity are qualitatively different than authorship and identity as they are formulated within a patriarchal framework. Identity is not a matter of defining herself against anybody, least of all the father; or of gaining distinction and recognition from those who are in a position of power and are hence a measure of value. Rather, her identity is formulated within a pact of mutuality with Madeline, an equally powerless woman, who is similarly "unimportant to anyone around her." But, as Stein was well aware, identity is a matter of re-collection and "sameness" as well as difference, a sameness secured over time through the establishment of consistency in one's past history. When Fanny tells Madeline her history, it is not her past which is so "important to her feeling," as the narrator repeatedly stresses, but the act of talking about it and Madeline's act of listening. The present participle is important—this is an activity which takes place in the present and is defined by present needs rather than the "objective" search for the truth of one's past. Thus, Fanny's act of authority is achieved not through a struggle based upon power relations and aggressive assertion. The "I" is immersed rather than distinct, almost an act of identification (mutual "ownership") formulated entirely in the present through attentive "talking and listening." Stein was later to elaborate upon this concept of "talking and listening" as crucial to her own enterprise as an author.

Having provided Fanny with a "listener," Stein's assertion that "I write for myself and strangers" seems at once defiant, in an important and necessary way, and bleak. This statement is not simply an acknowledgment that at this point "recognition" by a general audience was not feasible, but that her own immediate audience, which consisted primarily of her brother Leo and their immediate circle of mutual friends, was turning a deaf ear to her precarious and yet tenacious belief in the way she was expressing her own temperament and concerns. "I am important inside me and not any one really is listening" (p. 595), the narrator interrupts her narrative at one point to tell us. Though Gertrude and Leo's relationship consisted of genuine affection and a shared concern for intellectual and aesthetic endeavor, in actuality their relationship consisted of Gertrude's willingness to follow in the footsteps of her much admired brother. Leo, on the other hand, took it for granted that he was intellectually superior to his sister. His growing deafness was a physical handicap Gertrude soon exploited as a metaphor for his temperamental unwillingness to listen to others. With little concern for his listeners, Leo was egotistically fond of expounding upon modern aesthetics not only to his sister but to the group of people who gathered at the Stein's famous "Saturday evenings" to view their impressive collection of modern art. At these evenings Gertrude seemed content to play the observant and silent listener. After evenings spent in this manner, however, she sat writing until dawn, filling notebooks with her meditations upon the people she had observed, producing elaborate "diagrams" and groupings of them. Incapable himself of steadily seeing any one of his many projects or ambitions through to completion, Leo was both jealous of Gertrude's persistence and intellectually dismayed by her writing; his criticisms often reduced her to tears.

Leo's ridicule and disdain contributed to Stein's doubts about her writing, doubts which to some degree inform her faltering narrative style. On the one hand, Stein was quite sure that the only thing that made her want to "go on existing," and that gave her any sense of "importance" was her writing. On the other hand, she often disrupts the narrative to point out how much she wants to be understood, how she is often ashamed of her writing, and how much courage it takes to do "something no one is thinking is a serious thing." "While you are writing a book you are ashamed, you know you will be laughed at or pitied by every one and you have a queer feeling and you are not very certain and you go on writing" (p. 485). Stein develops a metaphor of economy—both psychic and monetary—to describe this "crazy" writing. Her writing is compared to her love of buying "bright handkerchiefs," which makes her like a "servant girl," since everyone else in her class "having good taste is using white ones or pale colored ones" (p. 487). Buying these bright handkerchiefs gives her a great deal of pleasure, which when denied causes much suffering. She is ashamed to buy them, yet they are an important consolation. Stein, who was fond of identifying her authority with the authority of servant girls, as we have seen in *Three Lives*, is both challenging the middle-class pleasure of the novel by her writing and offering a new consolation.

Stein, then, was capable of persisting despite doubts that she would be taken seriously or that she would be given immediate recognition. Far more important to her was the consolation she derived from creating for herself and "strangers" a new mode of perceiving people. This system is one her narrator expounds upon at length and that soon begins to inform the bulk of the book far more than do the individual "histories" of the Hersland family.

In the beginning of the "Martha Hersland" section, the narrator is so confident and enthusiastic about this system that her prose breaks into lyrical tributes to it. According to her summary, which she presents us with in this tribute, her system relies upon observing repetition and resemblance. "Everyone," she tells us, has a "bottom nature" which is always repeating. She allows herself "many years" of observing these repetitions and of waiting until she is "full up with completed being" before she can announce that "the whole being is clear." This observation is based upon "remembering" and allows her to group people according to "their kind of men and women." She is interested in establishing both the ways people resemble each other, and the ways in which they are individuals, different from each other. This learning process, she makes it clear both by her convoluted prose and many explicit statements, is very difficult. For example, one can mistake one particular mode of behavior as that person's "whole being," when, in fact, it might be a disguise for its opposite mode or simply a "piece" of the person. No observations, however apparently trivial or irrelevant, can be left out. But these difficulties make the endeavor more exciting, and the reward, "completed understanding," is not only "very satisfying" but "is to some all the meaning in their living" (p. 335).

The narrator's system is idiosyncratic only in its extremism. If human beings are constantly tempted to seek unifying concepts to protect themselves from the threat of constant diversity, and the center which will guarantee that unified structure, the narrator's ambitious attempt to conceptualize "everybody" could be looked upon as the almost Faustian extension of this attempt. The narrator's quest for everybody's "bottom nature"—the fundamental truth that lies at the center of our subjectivity—is a quest for a center that will guarantee unity, a "whole being." This idea of a bottom nature echoes the Platonic and Aristotelian concept of the soul, a substantial center that guarantees self-sameness through time, as well as insuring difference and a unique individuality. Yet, as Wendy Steiner points out, "the entire history of conceiving individuality has contributed to this elusiveness of 'pure individuality.' "[29] Steiner demonstrates the way in which conventions of portraiture, drawing upon Aristotelian premises, inevitably leads to the paradoxical merger of the individual with the type. This is precisely the contradiction the narrator confronts again and again in her attempt to create an ordered system for knowing everybody. "Everybody has their own being in them. Every one is a kind of men and women" (p. 333).

Despite its contradictions, the Aristotelian concept of the soul has persisted and perpetuated itself not only through the arts, but through firmly entrenched religious and psychological (both "commonsensical" and "scientific") beliefs. The Aristotelian concept of the soul, as John Wild has pointed out, "seems to support our desire for immortality, and this has certainly helped it to survive—as has its connections with Christian doctrines of divine retribution in an after-life. Such retribution would lose all meaning unless there were a substantial core of personality that could remain the same in surviving death [and that would guarantee] my unique responsibility for what I alone can do."[30] In *The Making of Americans*, Stein explores religion as a system of belief that infiltrates everyone's lives and allows them (especially if they are men) to establish their "sense of importance" and individuality. Her own methodology, of course, which relies upon her training in psychology under William James, shares this implicit connection with religion. More explicitly, however, her methodology relies upon the more rationalistic pursuits of nineteenth-century science and the methods upon which it thrived—observation, classification, categorization, and a firm belief in progress. Indeed, she had first proposed the system of characterization that she greatly enlarges upon in *The Making of Americans* in a published article on work she had done in a Harvard psychological study.[31]

In the 1903 fragment, Stein had proposed to use "kinds of people" and contrasts of character as a counterpoint to the way in which character is formulated by narrative plot and momentum. Typology was tentatively proposed as a "new beginning," an escape from patriarchal authority. Yet, when she begins to use this system again, in the first section of *The Making of Americans*, her "kinds of people" are all defined in terms of their relationships within the patriarchal family, i.e., in terms of modes of domination and subordination. Her quest for a "bottom nature" itself is a quest for a trait that "dominates," a governing personality trait that will operate hierarchically to determine the center of one's "whole being." In her notebooks, Stein even began to literally diagram groups of people as one would diagram sentence structure—into independent and dependent clauses, dominating leaders, perhaps, and their subdued followers.[32] Grammar, in a very literal way, structured her perceptions. However, as we have seen, her tenacious attempt to include women in this system only meant that the contradictions within her system become apparent. Women could only be individualized by being categorized as a "kind of person." And the terminology of these categories, moreover—"independent dependent," "attacking resisting," or vice versa—is radically ambiguous. Though Stein may have meant to suggest that in independent dependent people, for example, independence predominates, the oxymorons also suggest a dynamic interplay between elements instead of a stable governing essence. As her use of oxymorons reveals, Stein's "solutions" involve holding opposing possibilities in uneasy equilibrium. As she continues to put pressure on her solutions by tenaciously trying to make them work, she always finds the solutions dissolving in the very need to repose the question.

When she re-poses the question of her system by her explicit summary in the "Martha Hersland" section, she uneasily admits that in some people no particular characteristic at all "dominates them." These people, she asserts, are "in pieces" and "hold themselves together" only by acting, or "melodrama." After admitting an observation that could potentially undermine her ordered system, she immediately attempts to close off the question by the assertion that these people are "hardly not puzzling" (p. 312). Yet, as her wording suggests, she is barely capable of suppressing an interest in these people who are "in pieces." "When melodrama is taken from such a one then they remain confusing," she goes on to say, "there is nothing then to guide any one to know them as a whole then such a one. Such a one, now with no melodrama, just there as many pieces to some one, remains confusing. . . . They are in pieces to themselves then and to everyone. . . . So then such a one is puzzling" (p. 312).

Melodramatic performances are simply a matter of "pride" with these people, Stein tells us; they are "not natural." However, when she later defines her concept of "bottom nature," her metaphor of performance re-emerges in her definition, a definition qualified by language which, in and of itself, is not so melodramatic: "This is clear then, bottom being is the natural way of winning, loving, fighting, working, thinking, writing in each one" (p. 344). While the term "bottom being" is meant to suggest a "dominating trait," a fundamental stable essence and final hierarchical truth, her definition of that term indicates instead that she is interested in expressing styles of activity, modes of behavior. The words "bottom" and "natural" vie with the word "way," which suggests style, and with her use of verbals, which hold in equilibrium the function of both verb and noun, and thus suggest both stability and a fluid, dynamic sense of process and activity. Stein seems to be searching for a way to articulate a concept of being that would be a vital integration between the traditionally opposed dichotomies of Western thought: style and substance, appearance and a buried reality, stability and movement.

Similarly, her system, as she describes it, holds in equilibrium the possibility of both movement through time, and the culmination in description, a moment of stasis. Repetition, which can only be established in time, is yet the observation of sameness. Resemblances, both to one's own previous behavior, and to other people's behavior, is based on an act of recognition established through memory. The major requirement of her system, then, is that observations must be accumulated over a long period of time. One's "whole being" can not be announced as "complete" until all the evidence is in.

However, as she accrues more and more evidence the book must expand, infinitely. "This will be always then a longer and longer description always longer with my living and knowing" (p. 337). And if there is no precise cut-off point, no privileged instant of time where one can announce with certainty that a person is "complete," a point in time where this "being" falls into a neatly assembled package of a "whole history" then one's quest for "whole being" begins to look like a quest for the ever-elusive mirage of water upon the desert horizon. Stein can never find this point of finality, this privileged instant of time, since waiting simply means that more and more evidence, often contradicting her previous evidence and conclusions, comes in:

... each one sometimes is a whole one to me, then I am hearing or feeling or seeing some repeating coming out of that one that makes a completer one of that one, always then there may be sometimes more history of that one, there may never be a whole history of any one inside any one.... Slowly then that feeling is discouraging to one loving having a whole history of every one inside in one (p. 330).

The accumulation of evidence from patient waiting, moreover, vastly complicates her neat groupings of people:

... more and more I know where each one I am ever seeing belongs in the grouping, more and more then it all grows confusing, I am always knowing more and more and then it gets all mixed up in each one I am learning, each time there is in me a clear understanding of any one and I go on to another one or back to one I was earlier understanding that one is all a confusion from the last learning, each time then when there is a clear understanding of any one it is confusing with the next one, knowing more makes more grouping necessary in men and women and then all of a sudden this new grouping is a clear thing to my understanding and then sometimes all of a sudden I lose the meaning out of all of them I lose all of them and then each one I am then seeing looks like every one I have ever known in all my looking and there is no meaning in any of my grouping... (p. 335).

The narrator, however, does not immediately succumb to her confusion, feelings of discouragement, and doubts. Instead, she attempts to resolve her difficulties with the new evidence she garners through patient waiting, by beginning again and again. The narrator patiently, though with some anxiety and despair, allows the disintegration of a previous formulation as a new piece of evidence comes in, only to begin again with a new attempt to shape her knowledge into a composite, even more "complete," whole. To begin again allows her to include "new shades of repeating ... that I was neglecting" (p. 305), to backtrack to a previous starting point, and begin at that point again in order to expand the ensuing description by including more evidence. This activity of beginning again, however, is paradoxical, even as she describes it:

Always I remember every way one can hear only a part of it, the repeating that is the whole history of any one and so always I begin again as if I had never heard it.... Many times I begin and then begin again. Always I must not begin a deadened following, always their repeating must be a fresh feeling in my hearing, seeing, feeling (pp. 304-5).

How can she perceive repetition, which can only be established through memory, by acting as though she had never heard it before? The narrator clings to both the necessity for remembering even as she promotes the new possibility of not remembering, of ignoring previous starting points, goals, and intentions in order not "to begin a deadened following" but to remain true to a "fresh feeling" (p. 305). Each of these new beginnings would seem to promote difference and discontinuity, yet the narrator asserts that they can be recuperated: Every time she "begins again with listening," she tells us, it "slowly comes to a fuller sounding" and "then sometime everyone is a completed being in me" (p. 305).

In the process of trying to compose herself and everybody else, the narrator proceeds in a way which is only tenuously ordered. Movement forward, moments of faith, are met and hindered by relapses and doubts. Some sentences are repeated again and again, only to disappear before they can be developed. Other sentences are constructed by ignoring the punctuation—commas, semicolons, and periods—meant to separate and distinguish one phrase, or unit of thought, from the other. In this way some of her sentences never end; they simply run into each other. They seem to strain toward a fluid sense of continuing rather than a sense of completion. Accordingly, the act of completion becomes the anticipation of completion. "Sometime," the narrator promises again and again, "there will be a whole history" of this or that kind of person; and she often promises to write other books which will more fully explore a particular subject. Yet, time always brings the erosion of an idea, rather than its redemption. Her concepts dissolve in the very process of being defined; each moment of definition always suggests a "new way of feeling being." This new possibility is initially suppressed in the interest of clinging to an old formulation and vocabulary, even as the new idea changes the previous one beyond recognition, until the old formulation withers away completely and the new emerges and goes through the same process. This mode of beginning again and again suggests the process of living through history which Ortega y Gasset describes as a process of "being and unbeing":

Man invents for himself a program of life, a static form of being, that gives a satisfactory answer to the difficulties posed for him by circumstance. He essays this form of life, attempts to realize this imaginary character he has resolved to be. He embarks on the essay full of illusions and prosecutes the experiment with thoroughness. This means that he comes to *believe* deeply that this character is his real being. But meanwhile the experience has made apparent the shortcomings and limitations of the said program of life. It does not solve all the difficulties, and it creates new ones of its own. When first seen it was full face, with the light shining upon it: hence the illusions, the enthusiasm, the delights believed in store. With the back view its inadequacy is straightway revealed. Man thinks out another program of life. But this second program is drawn up in the light, not only of circumstance but also of the first. One aims at avoiding in the new project the drawbacks of the old. In the second, therefore, the first is still active; it is preserved in order to be avoided. Inexorably man shrinks from being what he was. On the second project of being, the second thorough experiment, there follows a third, forged in the light of the second and the first, and so on. Man "goes on being" and "unbeing"—living.[33]

The narrator describes her process of "being and unbeing," of beginning again and again, in terms of bodily sensations. She knows people by hearing, seeing, and then "feeling" them "inside" her; the rhythm of belief and disbelief is compared to the opening and closing of the hand—tenaciously gripping a belief and loosening that grip; and, more playfully, she associates the activity of accepting new knowledge and resisting it, and the activity of producing, composing, and telling about one's "whole being," to the process of ingesting, digesting, and to the retention and evacuation of the bowels. "This one was then a complete one to me, this one was then a solemn load inside me" (p. 320). When she is "filled up completely" with one's "whole being," she says, "then I tell it" (p. 323). "Sometimes it comes out of me I am filled full of knowing and it bursts . out from me, sometimes it comes very slowly from me, sometimes it comes sharply from me, sometimes it comes out of me to amuse me, sometimes it comes out of me as a way of doing a duty for me . . . sometimes very willingly out of me, sometimes not very willingly, always then it comes out of me" (p. 327).

Correspondingly, she begins to classify people's "bottom nature" in terms of "the way each one is made of a substance common to their kind of them, thicker, thinner, harder, softer, all of one consistency all of one lump, or little lumps stuck together," and the way this "substance acts in them" (p. 353). In doing so, she makes the same association of character traits with anal eroticism that Karl Abraham was to formulate as surviving in adulthood from the childhood developmental stage. In the first phase of this stage, "anal eroticism is linked to evacuation and the sadistic instinct to the destruction of the object."[34] Similarly, the narrator describes how she was "filled with the whole being" of one who was "a damned one to me." Being "filled" with the being of this one, she says, "gave to me the first meaning there was to me of the meaning of damning in all human religion. . . . I knew it then and I told it then to this one" (p. 324). In the second phase, "anal eroticism is linked with retention and the sadistic instinct to possession and control."[35] "Then the whole being of this one was inside me," the narrator says, "it was then as a possession of me. I could not get it out from inside me." Similarly, the narrator classifies people in terms of the "bottom attacking and the bottom resisting kinds of them," the "kinds of substance in them," and particularly the way in which these "kinds of people" relate to each other. One woman, for example, who has a "muggy resisting bottom" was "of the kind of woman that have to own the ones they need for loving" (p. 354). Those with "attacking bottoms," on the other hand, have moral convictions, a sense of superiority, and are opportunists who have "no instinct for quality in people but must completely understand and use them" (p. 364). The narrator's own impulse to classify, categorize, and tell about everyone based on her understanding of their "bottom natures" and "whole being," combines, as she seems to realize, the contradictory possibilities of anal eroticism: its potential for both creativity and loving but sadistic relationships. Sadism, Laplanche and Pontalis point out, is linked to anal eroticism because it "is essentially bipolar (since its self-contradictory aim is to destroy the object but also by mastering it to preserve it) and corresponds *par excellence* to the biphasic functioning of the anal sphincter."[36]

However, if the narrator classifies people according to this biphasic functioning, her classifications are, as usual, not stable. She becomes bewildered by, and bewildering about, mixtures and proportions of substances and natures; she feels one moment that it is "all a fabrication," the next moment, that it is a "certain thing." Through it all, she sees the "bottom nature" as, so to speak, active, struggling with other "natures" for domination. Finally, she arrives at the example of a man who will, she feels, wear himself out with "excessive spontaneous equilibration" (p. 377), an ambiguous state, since equilibration itself can be either static or dynamic. At this point she decides—wisely, perhaps, for the sake of her sanity—to "begin again" with the "history of Martha Hersland," who has been altogether ignored in the chapter devoted to her. Having reduced "bottom nature" to its most literal meaning as a "bottom substance," and to the way in which this substance is "active in them," the narrator begins to slowly relinquish her desire to discover a stable essence that would govern one's whole being, and all of one's activities. The narrator soon drops her terminology of "bottoms" altogether, and instead she emphasizes her search for one's "being," a verbal that was sometimes used in conjunction with "whole" as a noun, or with "bottom" as an activity or verb. To use "being" alone as a verb would be to lose all anchoring in static concepts and to make the attempt to convey movement in and of itself. The narrator, however, is not entirely ready for such a step.

Her interest in history, of course, would seem to provide an adequate vehicle to convey movement and change, but by the time she writes the "Martha Hersland" section she has preserved only a desultory interest in the progressive march from the past through the present to the future. Or, conversely, her belief in one's ability to either recuperate the past or project into the future is becoming more and more of a dead hypothesis. In the opening of *The Making of Americans* she had expressed her doubt that people ever feel their "age" inside them:

Indeed it is hard for us to feel even when we talk it long that we are old men and women or little as a baby or as children. Such parts of our living are never really there to us as present to our feeling . . . we never know ourselves as other than young and grown men and women (p. 5).

She sees this, she says, in the "stories told by old people" (p. 7). These people always tell stories about their past that in actuality speak to their present needs. Mr. Hersland tells stories about his "early living" in order to moralize to his children; Mrs. Hersland tells stories to Madeline in order to get the recognition and respect that her family fails to give her. The narrator, of course, is telling her history in an attempt to establish her identity and authority. However, when she is finally ready to begin Martha's history, her first statement is a revelation of her impatience and boredom with the notion of history:

This one was then once a very little one, a baby and then a little one and then a young girl and then a woman and then older and then later there was an ending to her and that was the history of this one (p. 386).

When she finally does fill in the details of Martha's history, she does so in a desultory fashion, interspersed with numerous digressions about various "kinds of people." The rather bored phrase, "as I was saying," serves as an indication that she is returning to the narrative line, and in this way she just barely manages to maintain a line of continuity, while the more intense excitement of beginning again begins to disappear.

As a child, Martha "wanted not to be existing" (p. 389). She makes one angry attempt to make people pay attention to her by throwing her umbrella in the mud; but despite her repeated announcements of what she had done the act goes unnoticed. Thereafter, she never tells anyone "what she is feeling inside her" (p. 413). She can never seem to please her father, who is often annoyed by and impatient with her, and her brother is assigned the task of taking care of her, an obligation he grudgingly accepts. Since "attacking is the natural way of winning" (p. 414), Martha never seems to win. "The being in her never got into motion to carry on to anything as object in attacking, it just remained inside her as knocking together in her to be a confusion and a nervous being in her . . ." (p. 414). The narrator links Martha's one childhood rebellion with her desire to go to college. After Martha witnesses a scene of aggressive violence—a man hitting a woman with an umbrella—she decides to leave Gossols and attend school in the East. At this point, the passive, ineffective Martha is simply given the character of Nancy in *Fernhurst*, and as a further indication, perhaps, of Stein's impatience and boredom, passages from that story are copied almost word for word.

Extending Martha Hersland's history by means of retelling

Nancy Redfern's experiences with her husband at *Fernhurst*, is, in a way, appropriate, for it completes Stein's autobiographical projection of herself in history, both forward, toward the future, and back, toward the past. But to project forward is, as Georges Poulet points out, a violent anticipatory movement wherein "the will [operates] to substitute for the undetermined future that is the work of chance, another future, predetermined, which is the work of the will."[37] Both the act of projection and the "project" demand the submission of the object of desirous observation to a predetermined plan. In discussing this sort of teleological discourse, Thomas Fries notes that it has the "a priori force of male aggression."[38] Stein's own use of projection, of this form of aggressive discourse is indeed a violent one. Both Nancy and Martha are projections of Stein's worst fears about herself for the future—that she will never be recognized, that she is stupid, and that she will always lose in any struggle for power.

However, Martha Hersland III's story also indicates the breakdown of Stein's projection of herself back, through genealogy. The story of the three generations of Marthas is a story of increasing debilitation and decline. Whereas Martha I was a strong matriarch who introduced the new by deploying the subversive strategy of leading by pleasing, and Martha II could "keep the world going" by cajoling her brother into an important step—getting married—Martha III is incapable of pleasing anyone, no matter how hard she tries. After Philip leaves Fernhurst, Martha spends her days studying hard so that she will be worthier of her husband in the event that he should return. He never does. Meanwhile, she has returned to her father's home and ends her days caring for a man who has only grown more irritable and impossible to please. Locating oneself in history seemed to indicate to Stein the necessary, unhappy, return to the father. The name Martha itself is an allusion to the biblical Martha, who located herself firmly within the realm of domesticity at the expense of developing her "inner life." Martha III's story, then, insists upon the inevitability of the return to the father and to the woman's traditional place within history, even while writing it seems to act as a kind of catharsis. Stein's intent to get rid of the story seems the most obvious thing about it. This impatience indicates Stein's weariness with writing and defining herself within a literary framework which not only seems to necessitate a feeling of authorial belatedness but also seems to demand a strategy of subversion while retaining a pleasing and familiar position.

Though she reveals an impatience with the narrative and history, Stein exploits the inappropriateness of including parts of *Fernhurst* within *The Making of Americans*. And what is inappropriate about transplanting her old story, *Fernhurst*, is its direct clash with the new style she is developing. Juxtaposed to the fluid style of *The Making of Americans*, the somewhat stiff and awkward nineteenth-century prose of *Fernhurst* simply seems like so much dead wood. Stein is briefly apologetic about it: "Some then have a little shame in them when they are copying an old piece of writing...." (p. 441) and follows this "old piece of writing" with a brief critique:

Categories that once to someone had real meaning can later in that same one be all empty. It is queer that words that meant something in our thinking and feeling can later come to have in them in us not at all any meaning. This is happening very often to almost every one having any realization in them in their feeling, in their thinking, in their imagining of the words they are always using. This is common then to many having in them any real realisation of the meaning of the words they are using. As I was saying categories that once to some one had real meaning come later to that same one not to have any meaning at all then for that one (p. 440).

Stein's introspective analysis of her own writing indicates her incipient acknowledgment of the twentieth-century recognition that language is a powerful system that formulates our categories of thought. When words are taken for granted they succeed in erasing not only their own arbitrariness, but the arbitrariness of the categories they have formulated for us. Maintaining arbitrary categories as natural is both the power and danger involved in the apparently neutral activity of language. As Michel Foucault points out, "there are conflicts, triumphs, injuries, dominations and enslavements that lie behind words, even when long use has chipped away their rough edges."[39]

Stein's critique indicates her new willingness not to take for granted what she had previously accepted in her earlier books: that conventional formulas and categories were inherently proper, natural, and right, and that language was simply a vehicle for transmitting the truth. By accepting conventional categories, she had aligned herself with those who were rewarded with proprietorship by the conventional system; she borrowed "propriety" from those whom she would have liked to criticize. This struggle was at least a live issue in *Fernhurst*. In *The Making of Americans*, where she announces in the beginning that her struggle against her own unconventionality was beginning to die away, she aligns herself with a new philosophy of "propriety," with those who do not simply repeat conventionally accepted forms and categories, for these were "empty" to her feeling, but with those who are "really feeling meaning in words they are saying" (p. 440). Stein returns with more conviction, then, to the proposition made in the beginning of her book, and acknowledges that what she is striving for is a poignant sense of "being," of what is alive to her present feeling. After acknowledging this, she promises to "begin again a description of Philip Redfern...using words having in my feeling, thinking, imagining very real meaning" (p. 441).

Since Philip Redfern had been expelled at the end of the *Fernhurst* narrative, the narrator's new beginning is essentially the act of reinterpretation, a new interpretation which will allow her to include what was previously neglected. She reinterprets Philip, then, as well as the three women characters of that story according to her new method of descriptive classification. All of one's characteristics, the narrator says, are "right in them," but other people "all think that one characteristic is the whole of them, they all forget the other things in them that are active in them, they all have it in common that in remembering anything they forget all the emotion they had then in them" (p. 442). The narrator advocates a decentered conception of character, sensitive to all one's characteristics without making a priority of any one of them and calling it one's "character." Her own enterprise is fed by the insatiable desire to know everything about everyone. In this enterprise, memory is both essential—one should not forget all their emotions—and problematic—one inevitably does. One forgets even in the process of remembering. This problematic activity of remembering, and her own asserted loyalty to her "present feelings" make her endeavor to describe one's "complete history," which suggests not only the complete knowledge of every characteristic but the recuperation of one's past, as well as the accurate projection of one's future, increasingly tenuous.

The narrator meditates upon these difficulties by meditating upon how one can "make mistakes in copying" (p. 454)—referring, perhaps, to her own activity of copying an old manuscript, as well as to the activity of description and the assumption of realism, that a real truth is to be communicated by producing resemblances. The narrator is ambiguously worried and tolerant about making mistakes.

Some seeing a mistake in their copying say then, oh how can I ever be certain, perhaps I have made many mistakes I have not been noticing. This is a sad thing . . . for always everyone is making mistakes and that is a very sad thing (p. 454).

Is the narrator sad that everyone makes mistakes, or sad that, having realized their mistakes, no one can be certain? Her own certainty is obviously at stake: "Perhaps no one ever gets a complete history of anyone. This is a very discouraging thing" (p. 454). And she professes that she is "despairing" at the notion of ever knowing one's "whole being" (p. 458).

Consequently, she meditates upon "successes" and "failures," only to decide that it is certainly "exciting" not to know with certainty the outcome of one's struggle:

And this is always and always a certain thing and always and always it is more exciting the knowing in one completely the character of them, the whole repeating in them, the whole range of being in them and yet not then being completely certain of them whether they will be succeeding or failing (p. 473).

This assertion suggests two contradictory possibilities: that the struggle in and of itself is important and not its endpoint or outcome, that is, whether it succeeds or fails, or, that the outcome is important but that the uncertainty and delay provoked by the necessity of waiting to discover it is exciting. The section ends in the ambiguity created by holding two options in equilibrium: the narrator seems to want to lose her sense of teleology and cling to it at the same time. Casting about for something to believe in, and to go on writing about, the narrator decides that "certainty" itself is "certainly very interesting" (p. 449), and the next chapter, "Alfred Hersland and Julia Dehning," proceeds with an investigation of the meaning of meaning. As the narrator's doubts about her ordered system become more excruciating in this section, her attempts to make her system work become more tenacious, even as she inevitably discovers in this very attempt a new beginning, a new mode of perceiving and creating "everyone."

"To begin again," then, is an activity that functions in several important ways in *The Making of Americans*. The act of beginning is an historical act, as the story of the first generation Herslands and their move to the new world indicates. But for the narrator the act of beginning is also the act of reinterpretation. Beginning again becomes a textual and stylistic strategy. This strategy arose out of the narrator's inadvertent, perhaps, but nonetheless highly inappropriate refusal to keep her mouth shut and proceed with the story. It allows her both to digress from, and to recuperate the narrative line. After each digression, however, it is impossible to proceed in exactly the same way; thus the very act of repetition—of repeatedly beginning again continuously promotes discontinuity and difference. To begin again and again is both to defer (to delay, and in that delay to submit to the hope of attaining closure) and to differ (from a previous formulation, which ironically makes closure provisional). The narrator, fed by the insatiable desire to know everything, and unable to rest easy with any complete formulation she attains, proceeds to turn the act of beginning again and again into a strategy for narrative survival.

The act of beginning is itself one of the most problematic acts of composition, for each beginning represents the attempt to select from the chaos of evidence a significant point and to make that point a priority. Stein, however, is too acutely aware of what is left out by this process of selection. "There are so many ways of beginning this description," she worries at one point. As the narrator wrestles with this problem of selection, she turns the struggle itself into a strategy for surviving it. By stylizing and repeating the act of beginning, she uses this compositional requirement against itself, for no one beginning is privileged, and beginning again and again always enables her to include more, particularly more of what was previously neglected. This is particularly important in terms of her attempt to include and to represent women's lives. Yet, because her methodology borrows from, and therefore preserves, some of the repressive measures of narrative teleology, the very attempt to include and represent women is always debunked and reversed against itself by the very women it is meant to include. This necessitates more new beginnings, and thus, the supplement ceaselessly supplants.[40]

Essentially, to begin again and again is not to begin at all. In his essay on Gertrude Stein, entitled "A Rose is a Rose . . . ," the French author Maurice Blanchot writes:

If what took place always comes back again and again, if what one said once not only does not cease to say itself, but always begins again, and not only begins again but imposes the idea on us that that has never really begun, having already from the beginning begun by beginning again, and through this destroying the myth of the original, then this movement links speech to a neutral movement of that which has neither beginning nor end, the incessant and the interminable.[41]

By beginning again and again, Stein was struggling to convey her idea of a "continuous present," a radically new mode of temporality that was not contingent upon origin or endpoint but upon the endurance of a dramatically flattened moment, sustained by return and repetition rather than accumulation and progress.

III. The Continuous Present

A thing not beginning and not ending is certainly continuing, one completely feeling something is one not having begun to feel anything because to have a beginning means that there will

be accumulation and then gradually dying away as ending and
this cannot be where a thing is a complete thing. (Gertrude
Stein, *The Making of Americans*, p. 701)

A noun is a repose. . . . A noun should always be replaced by now.
(Gertrude Stein, *How to Write*)

"Gertrude Stein has said some things tonight," Alice B. Toklas
once remarked, "that it will take her many years to understand." Similarly, Stein later recalled that she did not know
she was creating the "continuous present" while she was creating it, but that it had come to her "naturally":

. . . naturally I knew nothing of a continuous present but it came naturally to me to make one, it was simple it was clear to me and nobody
knew why it was done like that, I did not myself although naturally
to me it was natural.[42]

In the process of writing *The Making of Americans*, Stein was
forging one of her most important aesthetic principles; and she
was to spend the rest of her career exploring and explaining
its ramifications for writing. From the perspective of thirty
years later, she presents the process of creating the continuous
present as having been a "simple" and "natural" one. However,
The Making of Americans reveals a more agonizing and conscious struggle, a struggle with the conventional means of expressing and making sense. And it is her narrator's duty, the
duty of the self-conscious "I" of *The Making of Americans*, to
make sense of what, in a way, the text is already accomplishing.
The narrator's statements provide moments of stasis, moments
which halt the story in order for the narrator to remember
what she has been doing, what she will be doing, and where
she is going next:

I am always thinking I am not remembering what I am going to be
telling what I have been telling but really I am remembering pretty
well what I have been telling, what I am telling, what I am going to
be telling (p. 634).

The narrator tries to catch up, to acknowledge and conceptualize what she has already said, to project and understand

her project. The creation of the continuous present was both an inevitable and a conscious process.

Stein's "continuous present," then, is more fully understood in terms of her struggles with composition than in terms of the analogies critics often draw to William James's "ever moving present" or "stream of thought." There are marked similarities. James believed that "our total consciousness is constantly in transition and whatever may happen it never returns in its totality to the self-same condition."[43] Yet Stein never explains her continuous present in these terms, though she was fond of pointing out what she had learned from her favorite teacher. Her interests were, as she pointed out in her notebooks, aesthetic and compositional rather than philosophical.[44] Indeed, she received most of her philosophical ideas as they were filtered to her by her brother Leo, who was an even more avid devotee of both William James and philosophy. In her notebooks, she carefully recorded what she believed to be her point of departure from "pragmatism": "When Leo said all classification was teleological, I knew I was not a pragmatist."[45] Stein later explained that she learned the science of classification, a science she both utilizes and puts into question in *The Making of Americans*, while studying under William James.

When I was working with William James I completely learned one thing, that science is continuously busy with the complete description of something, with ultimately the complete description of anything with ultimately the complete description of everything.[46]

The point Stein wanted to make, however, was that a description could never really be "complete."

After all what does happen is that as relatively few people spend all their time describing anything and they stop and so in the meantime as everything goes on somebody else can always commence and go on. And so description is really endless.[47]

The "somebody else" who recommences in *The Making of Americans* is the narrator herself, who in the process of trying to compose herself and others can only find new ways to do it, who becomes, so to speak, another by constantly finding new points of departure. And since the narrator's quest for complete description, for a final stable truth, is the major drama of *The Making of Americans*, Stein begins to undermine both narrative teleology and classification by rendering this quest as a process of beginning again and again. Stein evolved the continuous present, in other words, in response to her difficulties and dissatisfaction with narrative teleology.

The process of beginning again and again tests the novel's creation of time as progressive, chronological, and accumulative. The sequential movement of the novel establishes, as Edward Said points out, a convention of finality: "neither what precedes each unit nor what follows it is considered equal to it at that moment." Sequential movement thus valorizes the conclusion, and behind this convention is "the imagery of succession, of paternity, of hierarchy."[48] The narrator is excruciatingly aware of how her novel is neither keeping time nor making sense in conventional ways: along with her penchant for buying "bright handkerchiefs," she tells us, she loves to buy "ugly clocks" (p. 487). This is serious business to her, though most people refuse to believe it. In this economic scheme, she considers the psychic economy as well by weighing the demands of the superego—the requirements of an internalized sense of the father's dictates—against not only her pleasure in these purchases but their inevitability despite her shame, i.e., their necessity as well. Her anxieties and uncertainties about her writing are transformed into a meditation on how other people establish meaning and certainty in their lives and how "unhappy" she is "that everyone is a little crazy."

There are several different ways of establishing certainty, the narrator tells us. Some do it by living up to other people's standards—they are part of a group and "need other people's company." Others need "a measure for it," like the people who "make a god out of their own virtue who sometimes is later a terror to them" (p. 480). Others, she says, "need drama to support it" (p. 479). It is hard to sympathize with all the ways people construct meaning in their lives, the narrator tells us. People are "crazy" because they adhere to their beliefs despite faulty logic or lack of verification from experience. Some people, for example, believe that a "river can not flow north because water can never be going up hill," and it takes "almost a quarelling to make them realise that north is not going up hill" (p. 496). Another woman, who is "very intelligent" and "well-read," nonetheless believes that "what happens every month to all women" only happens to women of the Plymouth Brethren persuasion (p. 495)—a deliberate poke on Stein's part at both the nineteenth-century taboo on mentioning menstruation, especially in novels, and at Puritanism, whose narrow-minded rigidity in matters concerning the body was one of Stein's favorite targets.

As the narrator tests the limits of the novel in order to include women's experience, she becomes bolder about transgressing the reticences surrounding the tabooed subject not only of menstruation but also of incest, though she still speaks euphemistically. The narrator tells a story of incest as one of two parables about father-child relationships, parables which expose the contradictions behind the father's activities if they are placed within the context of his own system of belief and morality. The father rationalizes his activity by the very system of morality which would forbid it. His need to believe in this rationalization, however, is shown to be a matter of life and death.

In the first parable, the father constantly writes letters to his daughter telling her that she should not do "things that were wrong that would disgrace him." After receiving several of these letters with this repetitive message, the daughter finally responds by telling him that he had no right to "write moral things in letters" since

he had taught her that he had commenced in her the doing the things that would disgrace her and he had said then when he had begun with her he had said he did it so that when she was older she could take care of herself with those who wished to make her do things that were wicked things and he could teach her and she would be stronger than such girls who had not any way of knowing better (p. 489).

The daughter's angry deflation of her father's rationalization causes him to become a "paralytic." "She is killing me," he tells his wife, Edith, and "he never wrote another letter" (p. 489). The patriarchal family (especially the middle-class Victorian family, where normal affections were intensified by confinement, resulting in "a hot-house atmosphere of intense domestic feeling"[49]) reinforces the taboo even as it creates the circumstances that invite its transgression. These transgressions are forbidden yet can be rationalized in terms of the existing moral code: "Some men do things because they are so good then they want every one to be wise enough to take care of themselves and so they do some things to them" (p. 489). Beginning with the same sentence of the father-daughter parable, the narrator proceeds to tell the parable of the father and his son who collects butterflies, a story with parallel theme: the father establishes a moral only to act in a contradictory fashion. The son's inheritance is to perpetuate the "cruel pleasure" of killing life in order to preserve it. Though he is "all mixed up inside him," he "goes on with his collecting" (p. 490).

Having exposed the contradictions behind the father's familial authority, the narrator herself becomes uneasy about how she is borrowing from this mode of authority. With increasing doubts and mixed feelings, the narrator goes on with what she now calls her "interesting collections" of kinds of people. This activity is a great comfort to her, she explains, though she realizes that it wouldn't be for everyone: she is seeing many people on the street who wouldn't be in the least bit interested. "Sometimes," she admits, "it is not an important thing inside me, sometimes it is a little dreary thing, making of everything that there is not anything inspiriting to be a live one" (p. 583). And her confusion reveals itself in the confusion of her categories. Alfred Hersland has in him "only one kind of being but as I was telling pieces of it get separated off from other pieces of it by not being completely acting, flavors, reactions, by-products get disconnected . . ." (p. 589). This makes her feel the whole business is "foolishness."

At stake is the narrator's own right to possess and control others by categorizing them. She regains her own self-possession and feeling that she is "a completely important one" by doing so (p. 587). The narrator, however, aims even higher than this: she cannot completely relinquish her desire for a hierarchy of importance. At once succumbing to the egoism of the system-maker, and challenging the strictures of the superego, the narrator immodestly hopes that reading her book will make other people wise, though "a little less wise than I who am the original wise one" (p. 708).

This proclamation co-exists with more democratic assertions: "In some way, anything, everything any one, every one says about any one is a true thing" (p. 576). And she admits that she does not have the control over her intentions, over the meaning she believes she is creating, that she had supposed: "Always in writing it, it is in me only one thing, a little I like it sometimes that there can be different ways of reading the thing I have been writing with only one feeling of a meaning" (p. 539). The narrator, of course, is always already generating pluralistic possibilities for meaning and new intentions not only for her readers but for herself, particularly by beginning again and again. She both resists and persists in finding new ways to produce meaning: "I am not very certain I am liking it that I am beginning in realising a quite new way to me of feeling living" (p. 621). There is no precise, single turning point—no one significant dramatic climax—in the narrator's quest for meaning, only constant change; and change, as her parable of the father and his children suggests, is vital, essential to survival. The father's sense of self-importance, grounded upon rationalization and a contradictory moral code, is so deeply entrenched and adhered to, that he becomes a "paralytic," unable to write any more, when his code of meaning and morals is challenged. Since her system allows her to establish a meaning which gives her a sense of self-importance, the narrator, likewise, has difficulties relinquishing it; yet her "new way of feeling being" begins to emerge more strongly in the "Alfred Hersland and Julia Dehning" section.

This new way of understanding people arises from the narrator's desire to experience what others are experiencing, and ironically, in a section devoted to a married couple, with the promiscuous desire to fall in love with everybody: "I would like certainly to be sometime in love with every one, to have every one sometime in love with me and then I would be certain what way each one had loving being being in them" (p. 658). Rather than directing her desire to know everyone into the more patriarchal and scientific mode of categorizing and classifying them, keeping them in the family, so to speak, the narrator advocates a more promiscuously loving attitude toward them. As the narrator moves from her reliance upon more rational, scientific endeavor and toward the more irrational endeavor to love everybody, she begins to strive as well toward understanding a more irrational mode of being than "meaning" or "certainty" (which she never rendered as being solely a matter of rationality anyway). This new mode of being is what she calls a "sense for living," a poignant, almost palpable sensation of life's exigencies. The narrator consequently becomes interested in talking about everybody's "sense for living," particularly in terms of those who have it and those who do not, and all the varying degrees therein.

The narrator begins her own meditation on a "sense for living" by announcing that "Dead is dead." The narrator elaborates upon death only by repeatedly insisting upon the phrase "to be dead is to be dead," and by associating it with men and their religion. There are some men—and she refers again, as an example, to the father of her parables—whose religion convinces them that "dead is not dead." This is a "generalized" and sometimes "sentimental" conviction; in some it is "a way of being important to themselves inside them... but always then they are really living the dead is dead living as a concrete living" (p. 499). For these men, in other words, the notion of an after-life co-exists with a way of life that does not rely upon belief in an after-life, and even contradicts such a belief. Rationalizing the value and pleasures of one's present, earthly life in terms of one's expectations for an after-life is the paradox encouraged by middle-class, Protestant religion, the religion of the "rich right Americans" Stein is writing about, and by the literary genre which arose out of this class and religion: the novel. If Protestantism prompted the habit of "interpreting every outward and inward occurrence for the sake of its spiritual significance," and insisted upon the "riches attendant to diligent spiritual enterprise,"[50] the narrator exposes the contradiction beneath the habit: it gives one a way of "explaining one's vices by one's virtues" (p. 500). To proclaim that "dead is dead," on the other hand, is to flatten metaphor (to insist upon absolute sameness: death is unlike anything but itself) in order to create a difference. This revitalizes, so to speak, the idea of death by divorcing it from its usual associations: as a moment of last reckoning or, with promises of an after-life and just rewards and punishments, associations that make death a moment of ritualized significance. Ritual comforts and familiarizes us with the mysterious and the terrifying. Thus its celebratory qualities, meant on the one hand to heighten significance, are always, on the other hand, in danger of becoming *too* familiar and therefore empty. The ritualized promise of an after-life, in particular, not only consoles us, it ultimately makes death insignificant: we will survive it.

Death is figuratively, or literally, the endpoint of the novel. Can one compose life without relying upon the anticipation of this endpoint and the meaning imposed by it, or conversely, without feeding upon the dead carcass of the past? Can one compose without killing in order to pin down, collect, re-collect, and preserve life? The problem posed to her by the parable of the father and his son's collection of butterflies, Stein later pointed out, brought her to acknowledge her "confusion of tenses"— the confusion of past and future with the present.[51] Roland Barthes points out that the past tense is the verb form *par excellence* of the nineteenth-century novel, a verb form

whereby the narrator reduces exploded reality to a slim and pure logos, without density, without volume, without spread and whose sole function is to unite as rapidly as possible a cause and an end ... the preterite is the very act by which society affirms its possession of its past and its possibility.[52]

The narrator has already analyzed and expressed her disinterest in the past, and stylized her new loyalty to her present feelings by her increased reliance upon the present participle. However, the endpoint of the novel functions to create meaning not only in terms of providing a privileged point of recollection and retrospection, but by giving us something to anticipate, a final resting point. In the traditional novel, time passing, or duration, is always given a meaningful orientation; each moment is a further revelation both of the author's intention and of a character's destiny. Thus time is teleological. A character is complete when we know the outcome of his destiny, which in retrospect explains and makes meaningful each of his actions, just as each event in his life is made contingent, continuous, and relevant. Of course, we must be given the illusion that each moment does not have its immediate justification, if any at all, just as our expectations for the final outcome must be foiled by several delays (which simply create more suspense and further whet our desire for the conclusion) in the interest of attaining a more complex solution. In the classical narrative, as Barthes points out, we are left with the sense that "truth itself is at the end of expectation."[53] It is the problem of anticipation that the narrator is particularly concerned with in the "Alfred Hersland and Julia Dehning" section. By further exploiting the present participle in order to emphasize delay and duration she both borrows from the narrative sense of time and begins to undermine it drastically.

The narrator's system borrows from narrative teleology in that her waiting periods, or delays, are initially meant to provide her with a fuller and more complex sense of truth and completion. Attaining the "truth" is obviously important to her, just as what she is doing reveals that this sense of certainty or completion is only a feeling of satisfaction, and a radically provisional one in her case. Never satisfied with any formulation she attains, she begins again and again and so her book expands, fed by an insatiable desire and the simultaneous hope that it will sometime be realized. In this section, particularly, she again and again anticipates the completion of her task: "I am coming again to be almost certain that I can sometime be writing the complete history of every one who ever was or will be living" (p. 665). She even anticipates writing more books in which, she promises, she will tell more about the history of her characters.

The narrator's sense of completion, however, is always foiled by the very strategy meant to attain it. In the "Alfred Hersland and Julia Dehning" section the narrator intensifies her effort to "wait" until she is filled up with "complete being" and she brings her loyalty to her present feeling to bear as a kind of test for a poignant sense of repletion. The reader, therefore, is given several minute to minute reports on how the narrator is doing in her "waiting to be filled." "I am completely now pretty nearly entirely now full" (p. 508), she announces, inventing an interesting stage of progress where one is "completely" almost close to completion. Yet she always counsels herself to be patient: "Still I am feeling some difficulties in the completion, they are not yet to me all of them entirely completely yet whole ones inside me, I am waiting and I am not yet certain, I am not yet impatient yet in waiting, I am waiting..." (p. 509). The narrator thus immerses the reader in the experience and the endurance of anticipation itself. Caught up in enduring and in rendering duration, the endpoint, what she is waiting for, begins to disintegrate. Alfred Hersland consistently falls into "pieces." Often the narrator worries that "everyone is in pieces inside me.... Perhaps not any one really is a whole one inside them to themselves or to any one" (p. 519). When she felt someone as a "whole one" before, she says, that was only because they were "anticipatorily suggestible" (p. 541). Now she announces, "Mostly just now I have a good deal of such feeling that every one is not a whole one that each one is not ever a complete one" (p. 543). The narrator's system for discovering a satisfactory unified concept of being disintegrates in the very intensity of her attempt to make it work.

Unity disintegrates in more than one way in this section, which is also devoted to a marriage, the symbolic union of antithesis. The marriage of Julia Dehning and Alfred Hersland is not a successful one, for their differences are never resolved. As the narrator retells and reinterprets this story, she renders their opposing modes of "being" in terms of her own dilemma: her contradictory impulse toward rendering duration on the one hand, and attaining completion on the other. Alfred aspires to be "completely full up with something" (p. 602). Julia "had very much excitement in being interested in each thing and continuing and being interested in some more thing" (p. 602). While Alfred does not have much "sense for living," Julia does, and is "certainly one being alive in living" (p. 654). Julia is constantly learning and striving, and is an "attacking" sort of person, while Alfred is a "resisting" one, "who was not learning anything from his being in living" (p. 601).

Julia's mode of "attacking," however, is also "resisting," for she "resists" learning a different way of attacking. While "she wanted a very much more earnest and exciting American living than the Dehning family living," she is inevitably pulled back toward it: "Julia was really then always of Dehning family living" (p. 650). It is partly because of her allegiance to "family living" that the marriage is not successful. In this respect, the family name Dehning is significant, for it is derived from the German possessive "Dein," and it is precisely because the Dehnings are so concerned about both their possessions and about how well Alfred will fit into their style of life that they can never accept him. The name Hersland, on the other hand, suggests both "her land" (a strong matriarchy), and the German word "herz," meaning heart or courage, and though this becomes increasingly ironic in the course of the novel, the Herslands have a pioneering spirit and the courage to take the very risks on new beginnings that the more bourgeois Dehnings fear. Julia and Alfred have two children, one of whom the Dehnings carefully decide looks just like them, but the marriage does not last. After much family discussion, the Dehnings decide that Alfred's business procedures, carried on by means of money borrowed from Mr. Dehning, are too risky: he does not spend money wisely or "honestly" enough. Julia and Alfred separate; Alfred remarries while Julia does not.

The narrator renders this story far differently than she did in the 1903 fragment. In the 1903 fragment, Mr. Dehning was origin, endpoint, and pivot upon which the story rotated; in this rendition, though he is still responsible for creating a sense of Dehning family living, he is no longer the transcendentally wise one, but simply one who likes to listen and advise and who is fairly happy and content in his "rich right American living." The story of Julia's struggle with her father, a struggle which put her in the position of both rebelling from and ultimately submitting to her father, is deleted entirely. Though both the father and the narrator still pronounce final judgment, there is much family discussion in the story, and the narrator's own assessment of the marriage is more tolerant. Instead of proclaiming Julia and Alfred's marriage a mistake, if not a disaster, the narrator now decides that it "was alright from the being in them that Alfred and Julia should come to be loving one another and marrying and not succeeding in their daily living."

The narrator, then, does not bring her story to an abrupt halt with a consideration of the disastrous effects of Julia's marriage. Instead, the narrator develops and sustains a new beginning, a new mode of expressing "being" by rendering Julia's life after her marriage to Alfred. This new mode is the narrator's first conscious attempt to create a sense of going on, of continuing without beginning or end. It is increasingly verbal—in both senses of the word—for it is both heavily reliant upon verbs and verbals, and is incredibly verbose, like Mrs. Dehning "who was certain to be talking on and on to herself and to Julia and to everyone in Dehning family living who was then not listening" (p. 689). Once again, the narrator develops a new mode of expression by identifying with and including the outsider, in this case the mother who is somewhat of a family extra, and never really listened to. In discussing the development of her "continuous present," Stein later said that she was striving for a sense of "evenness," and that she did this by dropping "dependent clauses" and punctuation—any element of grammar that would not only disrupt a sense of fluid duration but that would create hierarchy or give directives to the reader, whom Stein considered well enough able to decide when he or she wanted to take a breath. She was striving for this evenness, in other words, out of a democratic impulse, the impulse to "give everyone a vote"[54] (and a voice in the creation of meaning). Just as women had been given the vote in the twentieth century she remarked, so too should children, because once one was conscious one had a stake in what was going on.[55]

And "going on" is literally the way she renders Julia's "being." Julia was "one certainly going to be from being in her one going to be going on being one going to be living" (p. 691). The narrator plays on the capacity of the word "going" to suggest both duration, or "going on" and what is "going to" happen.

Thus the idea of a future and the possibility of anticipation is retained, but only as it is felt in an enduring present; and after all, she can only expect to be "going on": she is "going to be going on." This means of rendering being, in other words, absolutely flattens dramatic significance and is not contingent upon origin or endpoint. Death is radically discontinuous: "When she was ending she would come of course to be one not any longer being in living but that would be simply that she had come then sometime to be a dead one, not that she had ever come to be one not going on being one going on being living" (p. 686). This literal-minded, wordy, and wearying march of verbs and verbals could be considered an unfortunate way of conveying her "sense for living" and "continuous present." Her "Beethovian passages," as Stein later referred to them, are hardly likely to seem Beethovian to the reader, who is more likely to be put to sleep by them. However, the allusion is appropriate and fair if we take into account Stein's excitement, and her intensely passionate struggle not only to challenge the strictures of patriarchal discourse, but to create an alternative. She had talked herself out of trying to please the father, or live up to his standards to attract an audience. With a great deal of concentrated commitment and excitement, and not much concern for her readers' conventional pleasure and degree of patience, Stein continued to explore the potential of this verbal-laden prose in her "Portraits," which she was writing at the same time as *The Making of Americans*.

At the end of the "Alfred Hersland and Julia Dehning" section the narrator announces that she is no longer writing for anyone, not even for herself. She is writing, not in search of anything, or in terms of any particular goal such as identity or recognition, but instead with a sense of being somewhat out of control and uncertain, and because writing is her way of going on living. Just as she had rendered Julia as "going on living," the narrator renders her task as one of "going on writing." "So then I will go on writing and not for myself and not for any other one but because it is a thing I certainly can be doing with sometimes exciting feeling and sometimes happy feeling and sometimes almost indifferent feeling and always with a little dubious feeling" (p. 708).

The narrator's narrative—the story of her quest for knowledge, for the discovery of everyone's "whole being" and "complete history" comes to an end in the beginning of the "David Hersland" section. Her eyes, she tells us, are "large with needed weeping" because she realizes that she can not experience what everyone is experiencing and know everything there is to know (p. 729). Yet her desire to know everything completely—the desire that kept her quest alive—is not acknowledged as a "mistake." Although she has been "wrong" she does not feel remorseful. Instead, she claims to have learned even more from her "mistakes" and that making them has made her a "joyous wise one" (p. 573). Thus, she does not punish herself, as she had earlier punished Julia by dooming her to a miserable existence for making the mistake of rebelling against the father's "keen completed look" and wandering outside Dehning family living. Indeed, the narrator's "wisdom" was only attained by wandering away from the father's and the novel's traditional line of succession, by following inclination rather than the dictates of reason and her duties as a narrator.

Consequently, while the traditional narrative quest ends with the discovery, and/or appropriation of the father's name, the narrator's quest ends with the consideration of "illegitimacy." "I do ask some if they would mind it if they found out that they did not have the name they had then . . . if they had been born illegitimate" (p. 723). The narrator might be politely inquiring of those very people she is observing in order to understand and write about, whether they would mind being created by the narrator's new mode of authority, which is not only relying less and less upon names and nouns but is, by this time, becoming increasingly illegitimate. Her question is a bit coy, of course, for she has already begun to disinherit both herself and the characters she creates from the name of the father and his line of succession, and to own and create their "being" in a new way.

Naming is not only a way of designating to whom one belongs, to what class, kin, or kind, but is also a way of understanding by possessing, conceptualizing, and labeling. Similarly, an author's act of naming is the act of bestowing significance and destiny. By way of explaining her adversion to names,

Stein later pointed out that they were not so important when you really loved someone or something, for then you rarely called them by their name. In *The Making of Americans*, the names of her major characters become increasingly ironic, as each name's significance is either drained or reversed upon itself. Just as the name of the women on the paternal side, "Martha," designates a "woman's place," the name of David is an allusion to the Old Testament king who slew Goliath, superseded the jealous Saul, and became a popular king and good father. However, just as the story of the Marthas of the family becomes, finally, the story of a woman who fails in her domestic duties, the story of the Davids becomes the story of decreasing vitality, potency, and ability to be a good father.

David I sincerely wanted to do what was best for his "many children," but had to be prodded by his wife into making a successful transition to the New World, where he is comfortably prosperous and is able to leave his wife "a nice little fortune." David II is "full up with beginning," a pioneer who takes his family to the "newest part of the new world." Yet, fascinated more by his own ideas and theories of education than by their value to his three children, he becomes increasingly domineering—an impatient, irritating, and annoying man, whose children mostly live in fear of him. He is left at the "end of his middle living" when he begins to lose his "great fortune," and to "shrink away from the outside of him." David III, to whom the last chapter of the book is devoted, "never really wanted to be needing to have much feeling about having babies in being living. He did not have any of them" (p. 793). David III is "dead," the narrator tells us, "before the ending of the beginning of his middle living" (p. 740).

If, by the last chapter, the vitality is completely drained from the "name of the father" and from the genre which his name legitimates and guarantees, the narrator returns to the possibilities latent in the maternal line, and the way Fanny Hissen established her act of authority by "listening and talking." Acknowledging again her difficulties with, and disbelief in, "realising the whole being, having been, going on, the going to be going on in anyone," the narrator says she is no longer "thinking about doing this thing" (p. 732). Instead, "I am think-

ing then about telling about knowing being being in men and
women. I am thinking then about listening and talking being
..." (p. 732).

Since the narrator decides to proceed in the name of the
mother, rather than the father, the name "Fanny Hissen" should
be discussed as well. "Fanny," a perfectly typical nineteenth-
century woman's name, also alludes, of course, to the narrator's
own quest for the bottom—absolute certainty as well as "bottom
natures"—a quest that initiates, in the "Martha Hersland"
chapter, the narrator's first major digression from the narrative
line of family history, and turns the narrative inside out. Unlike the names Hersland and Dehning, which are derived from
German words, "Hissen" is, in and of itself, a German word—
a verb meaning to hoist or raise, and used particularly with
the word flag. This name, then, signals both Stein's love of
turning the noun (the name) into a verb, and her attempt to
raise herself by keeping close to her roots. Stein's own language, beginning in *Three Lives*, relies a great deal upon the
colloquial English of the German immigrant, especially her
use of the present participle[56] which is increasingly stylized
and serves the function in *The Making of Americans* of setting
her free from the determinations of the past, the "substantive
act" of the novel. In the last chapter the prose moves almost
entirely by means of participles. Just as the vitality of the
father's proper name is drained, so too is the vitality of the
noun. Whereas the three preceding chapters were filled with
proper names, in this chapter both proper names and nouns
almost entirely disappear, to be replaced by ones, someones,
somes, everyones—to be replaced, in other words, by the indefinite pronoun.

The last chapter of *The Making of Americans*, then, suggests
the death of the novel, a genre which thrives upon the name
of the father, and the belief that individual experience and
sensory data, provided especially by the eye, were the very
substance of reality. If David's individuality is overwhelmed
by indefinite pronouns and by a typical narrative strategy which
renders the experience of "somes" and delegates David to being
"such a one," the narrator's quest for her own individuality
and identity ends with the disappearance of the "I" and the

eye of the narrator. The narrator has developed a case of eye-strain, anyway, from "looking and looking and looking" at everyone; and she has suggested that the aggression behind the look that turns into a stare is the aggressive attempt to find resemblances and sameness rather than difference. The metaphoric language of producing meaning by the penetrating and "keen completed look" of the father is exchanged for the more amorphous and receptive mode of "listening and talking."

"Listening and talking," Stein later explained, is a mode of authority that does not presuppose resemblance, and thus does not necessitate remembering; therefore it does not function to create identity.[57] Stein thought that it was rather easy not to have an identity, for when one is in the act of doing anything, one does not think of it.[58] The artist, for example, caught up in the intensity and excitement of the activity of creation does not think of remembering—either what he has done and is going to do, or what his audience will recognize or understand. Doing so produces writing that is lifeless and dull, and will not survive.[59] Yet not writing in this way is extremely difficult, Stein pointed out, because while it is not difficult to not have an identity, *knowing* that one does not have an identity is extremely difficult. It is our conceptual apparatus, in other words, that functions to create and reinforce identity. This does not mean that Stein scorned conceptual understanding, although she was constantly wary of how it could divorce one from the immediacy of actual experience. Rather, she saw the human mind as capable of play and infinite possibility. It was her self-appointed task to change the mind, not to ignore it.

In this respect, the mode of "listening and talking" might be applied to Stein's idea that there is no such thing as repetition in living. Things are only perceived as the same on a more abstract level of conceptual understanding. For the idea of repetition, Stein substituted what she called "insistence," or "moment to moment emphasizing" that was always different, no matter how minute this difference was. When we see this "moment to moment emphasizing" on the page, it may look the same, but our emphasis in saying it will always be different and produce difference. Insistence is a function of speech, and can better be heard than seen. Stein, then, was not simply opposing difference to sameness. Everything is so much the same, she once remarked, that it is simply different.[60] Creating difference by insisting upon absolute sameness was one of her favorite strategies, as can be demonstrated in her proclamation that "dead is dead" in *The Making of Americans*, and in her later infamous phrase "a rose is a rose is a rose is a rose."

The last chapter of *The Making of Americans* proceeds by "listening and talking," and is Stein's first attempt to write without an "I." Without an I to disrupt the flow of the narrative by announcing what she will do, what she has been doing and what she is doing, and her problems with all of these activities, the narrative moves more fluidly. However, the I does not disappear in order to go into hiding; the principle of identity is gone completely. Thus, the text proceeds in what seems to be an arbitrary way, without either an I or eye to give us perspective, continuing without continuity, without any concern for consistency, chronology, or cause and effect. And in terms of creating David's "being," this mode of "listening and talking" implies a reciprocal relationship, an act of authority based not upon the discovery of an identity but upon an act of sympathetic identification.

In this respect, it is significant that both the narrative "I" and David are pronounced dead at the same point. Bridgman argues that David is modeled upon Leo, and while this seems plausible, the chapter clearly conflates much of Gertrude's own experiences (rendered before by the narrative I) with Leo's in order to render David's.[61] David is the youngest in the family—Gertrude's position, shared by Leo, who was two years older. David, like Gertrude and Leo, was born to take the place of two other children who had died, a fact that made him feel his existence peculiar and accidental, just as it did Gertrude and Leo. David, like Gertrude and Leo, leads the life of an intellectual: His "being existing" is rendered almost entirely in terms of mental qualities—thinking, remembering, knowing, forgetting, listening, meaning, being logical, being convincing, explaining and expressing things clearly. This "being existing" evolves into a kind of excruciating self-consciousness. Thinking and its relationship to experiencing is one of the issues upon which the "two living together" in this chapter part ways. David's death speaks, in one respect, to the end of Gertrude and Leo's shared life, shared perceptions, and even shared identity. The two living together co-exist peacefully enough at times, though there is a sustained meditation upon quarrelling, angry feeling, and even "completely furious angry feeling." The differences, however, are announced more calmly and are not simply the cause of this angry feeling.

Some one was not having angry feeling when he was asking why any one is doing anything. This one did not have angry feeling when he was asking why any one is doing anything. This one did not have angry feeling when some one was explaining that each one did the thing that each one was doing so as to be satisfying the wanting to do that thing that each one had then inside in them (p. 813).

The repeated question and explanations make it clear that the "someone" is not convincing David. What this "someone" is doing is later done and announced as a "complete thing," but David was not "gently seeing it as a complete thing." David "was certain that really one of them was the more important one" (p. 779). While "some certainly are wondering if deciding anything is giving any meaning in being one being living," and "are certainly uncertain whether they should have a feeling of submission when some one has decided something," David perceives himself to be a clearer thinker and more decisive, though the prose hints that his decisiveness and thinking lack a certain vigor and vitality: "He was deciding about thinking clearly about clearly thinking about the things about which he was thinking" (p. 855). David, it seems, recedes from immediately felt experiences or ideas into the potentially infinite regression of the mind. He can not simply think about something, but must think about thinking about it. Rather than being interested in something, he is more often "interested in being interested." David's lack of vigor and vitality becomes increasingly evident. While "some who are in the ending of the beginning of their middle living are then seeing changing existing in every one who is being living," David Hersland "was realising all his living that changing is existing in every one and he was not really feeling this thing. . ." (p. 844). Toward the end of the chapter, David stops feeling changing in his existing and being interested in "beginning again" entirely. David is then both figuratively and literally dead in his middle age.

The differences between the "two living together" are never resolved nor evaluated, only presented and proliferated in a remarkably even voice. Even after David is dead and "buried" no judgment is passed though all the remarks that "some" make about him are recorded. The final decision rests with the reader, and thus suggests one final implication of writing with no identity. "If there was no identity no one could be governed," Stein later remarked.[62]

And so the book ends. In the coda, entitled "History of a Family's Progress," the narrator goes on proliferating possibilities rather than progressing toward a resolution. Some may go on existing in family living. "Certainly they may be in family living. . . . Certainly they may not be in any family living. They may be in the family living they are then having. They may not be in the family living they are then having" (p. 917). And so it goes. Indeed, it is difficult to imagine how a text which insists upon enduring by going on in this fashion could ever create a conventional sense of an ending. The last issue the narrator must "decide" upon is whether anyone will remember family living. Again, "there can be some who are not completely remembering such a thing," and some who "can remember something of such a thing" (p. 925). Thus, deciding how important family existing is, is left up to the reader's discretion. Family existing may go on, and some will not remember it, while some "can remember" it. As for Stein herself, she was later fond of saying "if it can be done, why do it?" If the last sentence of her novel is not exactly a dramatic resolution, Stein did suggest a new reason for closure: "Anyway," she later remarked, "you always have to stop doing something sometime."[63]

Stein did not go on remembering "family living," or borrowing from it in her writing as a paradigm of explanation. She later claimed that she wanted to do what she was doing so completely in *The Making of Americans* that she would lose

it—lose, in other words, both the scientific and literary prac-
tices of the nineteenth century which relied and thrived upon
a belief in reason, progress, and patriarchy. As with her characters in *The Making of Americans*, this loss was an important
awakening. This release from the nineteenth century, from
patriarchy and rationality, was a vital source of energy for her,
to which her voluminous output over the extent of her career
attests. Having lost the nineteenth century, she never expressed any regrets or nostalgia for it; instead she became an
ardent advocate for the twentieth century. "So then the twentieth century is a splendid period, not a reasonable one in the
scientific sense, but splendid."[64]

For after all, the "great author's" task, as Stein saw it, was
to completely live in and express the present. But just as this
present is constantly changing, so too was Stein's way of rendering it. Having struggled so hard to release herself from the
principle of identity, Stein continued to create difference, to
create meaning and compose herself and others in new ways,
to begin again and again. There is perhaps no other writer who
was so thoroughly experimental, who created as many different
styles over the course of his or her career, as Stein.

Thus, the "continuous present" is not simply her way of rendering it by means of duration and the present participle in
The Making of Americans. This style emerged out of her difficulties and objections to narrative teleology, just as her use
of the word "being" borrows from the vocabulary of classical
philosophy, even if Stein finally disagreed with its classical
definition as a transcendental and unchanging essence. It may
be impossible, moreover, to render being without thinking of
origin and death. Since one of the major functions of language,
of normal syntax, is to predicate, the notion of origin and death
may be built into the language. Stein, however, never gave up
challenging that function of language, or challenging our need
for, or use of, normal syntax. Thus, after completing *The Making of Americans* and her portraits, she creates her "continuous
present" in *Tender Buttons* by taking in an origin in a poem
in the "Food" section entitled "Orange In" and proceeding to
"excreate" (to excrete and create out of it) "a no, a no since, a

no since when, a no since when since, a no since. . . ."[65] A "no since" is not precisely nonsense, though it is obviously meant to sound like it.

By producing much more no since, no since when (no cause and effect, no originating event) Stein continued to analyze and challenge our old ways of thinking and to suggest different connections, to produce meaning in new ways. If the impetus for this analysis and challenge was initiated by her objection to both silence and to her position as a woman in patriarchy, in a way it continued by exploiting that very position. *Tender Buttons*, for example, not only exploits and celebrates the realm of domesticity, but her title could suggest not only new and vulnerable connections, but parts of the woman's body as well—the nipples, the clitoris. More extensively, Stein's writing relies upon exploiting the very nature of woman's traditional position—her "silence," her seeming "nonsense." Stein's writing, despite her voluminous output produced by years of concentrated and careful talking and listening, was not seriously listened to very often, and remained incomprehensible to even some of her most ardent admirers. Her reputation grew as a sort of spectacle, as friend and patron of famous artists and subject of their portraits, as "Mother Goose" and the "Sybil of Montparnasse." This, however, is changing, and with good reason. For what is at stake in learning how to attend to those silences, in learning how they function, is access to a shrewd analysis of the authority of patriarchal discourse, and an alternative to it.

Notes

Introduction

1. Gertrude Stein, *Fernhurst, Q.E.D., and Other Early Writings by Gertrude Stein* (New York: Liveright, 1971), p. 132.

2. Gertrude Stein, *Everybody's Autobiography* (New York: Random House, 1937), p. 123.

3. *Gertrude Stein: Writings and Lectures 1909-1945*, ed. Patricia Meyerowitz (Baltimore, Md.: Penguin Books, 1971), p. 200.

4. Gertrude Stein, *Geography and Plays* (New York: Something Else Press, Inc., 1968), pp. 34, 92-93, 205.

5. Quoted by Samuel Stewart, *Dear Sammy: Letters from Gertrude Stein*, ed. Samuel Stewart (Boston: Houghton Mifflin Co., 1977), p. 57.

6. Quoted by James Mellow, *Charmed Circle: Gertrude Stein and Company* (New York: Avon Books, 1975), p. 417.

7. *Writings and Lectures 1909-1945*, p. 198.

8. *The Pound Era* (Berkeley: University of California Press, 1971), p. 23.

9. *Three Novels by Samuel Beckett* (New York: Grove Press, 1955), p. 414.

10. Susan Sontag, *Styles of Radical Will* (New York: Dell Publishing Co., 1969), pp. 3-34.

11. See Neil Schmitz's fine discussion of Gertrude Stein's humor in his book, *Huck and Alice: Humorous Writing in American Literature* (Minneapolis: University of Minnesota Press, 1983), especially pp. 160-239.

12. Michael Hoffman, *Gertrude Stein* (London: George Prior Publishers, 1976), p. 17.

13. Richard Bridgman, *Gertrude Stein in Pieces* (New York: Oxford University Press, 1971), p. 7.

14. Ibid., pp. 79, 61.

15. Ibid., p. 90

16. Wendy Steiner, *Exact Resemblance to Exact Resemblance* (New Haven: Yale University Press, 1978), p. x.

17. Michel Foucault, *Archaeology of Knowledge*, trans. A. M. Sheridan Smith (New York: Pantheon Books, 1972), p. 218.

18. Ibid., p. 219.

19. William Gass, "Gertrude Stein: Her Escape from Protective Language," *Accent*, 18:4 (Autumn 1958), 233-44. Gass focuses upon Stein's most hostile critic, B. Reid, and his book, *Art by Subtraction*.

20. *The History of Sexuality, Vol I: An Introduction*, trans. Robert Hurley (New York: Vintage Books, 1980), p. 27.

21. Henry James, *The Wings of the Dove* (Columbus, Ohio: Charles E. Merrill, 1970), p. 156.

22. Gertrude Stein, "Gertrude Stein Talking—A Transatlantic Interview," *A Primer for the Gradual Understanding of Gertrude Stein*, ed. Robert Bartlett Haas (Santa Barbara, Calif.: Black Sparrow Press, 1976), p. 18.

23. Bridgman, *Gertrude Stein in Pieces*, p. 67.

24. Catherine Stimpson considers Gertrude Stein's conflict between her sexuality and her intellectual ambitions; see "The Mind, the Body and Gertrude Stein," *Critical Inquiry* 3:3 (Spring 1977), 489-506. Marianne DeKoven's book, *A Different Language: Gertrude Stein's Experimental Writing* (Madison: The University of Wisconsin Press, 1983), published after this book was completed, offers an exciting analysis of Stein's later writings from a feminist and post-structuralist perspective.

25. Gertrude Stein, *The Geographical History of America* (New York: Vintage Books, 1973), p. 218.

26. Stein, *Fernhurst, Q.E.D., and Other Early Writings*, p. 58.

27. Several French feminists, in particular, have observed that the aims of feminist discourse would intersect with the aims of a post-structuralist challenge to the "phallocentric" discourse of Western culture. In effect, they call for an alternative language that would emphasize the viability of difference (defined as difference *within*, or the non-coincidence of the subject with itself), fragmentation, non-mastery and dispersal as subversive of identity and dichotomous oppositions. See Luce Irigaray, *Speculum of the Other Woman*, trans. Gillian C. Gill (Ithaca, N.Y.: Cornell University Press, 1985) and *This Sex Which Is Not One*, trans. Catherine Porter (Ithaca, N.Y.: Cornell

University Press, 1985). For an introduction to Irigaray and other French feminists, see *The New French Feminisms*, ed. Elaine Marks and Isabelle de Courtivron (Amherst: University of Massachusetts Press, 1980), which includes translations of excerpts from Irigaray's and other French feminists' writings.

28. Foucault, *Archaeology of Knowledge*, p. 219.

29. Josette Feral "Antigone or the Irony of the Tribe," trans. Alice Jardine and Tom Gora, *Diacritics* 8:3 (September 1978), 5.

30. Jean E. Kennard, *Victims of Convention* (Hamden, Conn.: Archon Books, 1978).

31. Leo Bersani, *A Future for Astyanax: Character and Desire in Literature* (Boston: Little, Brown and Co., 1976).

Chapter I

1. Quoted by Samuel Stewart, *Dear Sammy: Letters from Gertrude Stein*, ed. Samuel Stewart (Boston: Houghton Mifflin Co., 1977), p. 57.

2. Leon Katz, "Introduction" to Gertrude Stein, *Fernhurst, Q.E.D., and Other Early Writings by Gertrude Stein* (New York: Liveright, 1971).

3. Gertrude Stein, *The Autobiography of Alice B. Toklas* (New York: Random House, 1933), pp. 84-85.

4. Leon Katz, "The First Making of *The Making of Americans*: A Study Based on Gertrude Stein's Notebooks and Early Versions of Her Novel," Diss. Columbia University 1963, p. 16, n.1.

5. *Staying on Alone: Letters of Alice B. Toklas*, ed. Edward Burns (New York: Liveright, 1973), p. 63.

6. Katz, "Introduction," p. xi.

7. Ibid., pp. xi-xli.

8. Ibid., p. xli.

9. J. Hillis Miller, "Narrative and History," *ELH*, 41:3 (Fall 1974), 456.

10. Ibid., p. 459.

11. Ibid., p. 473.

12. "Autobiography as De-facement," *MLN*, 94:5 (December 1979), 920.

13. Linda Simon, *The Biography of Alice B. Toklas* (Garden City, N.Y.: Doubleday and Co., 1977), p. 181.

14. Gertrude Stein, *Fernhurst, Q.E.D., and Other Early Writings by Gertrude Stein* (New York: Liveright, 1971), p. 64. All citations are

to this edition and will hereafter be included in parentheses in the text.

15. Dante Alighieri, *La Vita Nuova*, trans. Mark Musa (Bloomington: Indiana University Press, 1971), p. 30.

16. Ibid., p. 30.

17. Ibid., p. 86.

18. Ibid., p. 20.

19. See John Malcolm Brinnin, *The Third Rose* (Boston: Little, Brown and Company, 1959), p. 46; Michael Hoffman, *The Development of Abstractionism in the Writings of Gertrude Stein* (Philadelphia: University of Pennsylvania Press, 1965), pp. 34-35; and Carolyn Faunce Copeland, *Language and Time and Gertrude Stein* (Iowa City: University of Iowa Press, 1971), pp. 10-16.

20. Henry James, *The Wings of the Dove* (Columbus, Ohio: Charles E. Merrill, 1970), pp. 10-16.

21. Ibid., p. 42.

22. Ibid., p. 44.

23. Ibid., p. 56.

24. Ibid., p. 84.

25. Ibid., p. 156.

26. In a letter of 1947 to Donald Sutherland, Alice writes: " . . . in 1903 in a novelette (which was the point of departure for "Melanctha"—the three characters are white) she quotes Kate Croy. . . . But in rereading *The Wings of the Dove* there were suddenly some very direct connections between Kate Croy and Melanctha—between Gertrude's dialectic and his. It fascinated me. It was the only book I remember her having reread several times." Toklas, *Staying on Alone*, pp. 86, 84.

27. Stein, *The Autobiography of Alice B. Toklas*, p. 78.

28. Harold Bloom, *The Anxiety of Influence* (New York: Oxford University Press, 1973), pp. 99, 107.

29. Ibid., p. 26.

30. Toklas, *Staying on Alone*, p. 86.

31. Shoshana Felman, "Turning the Screw of Interpretation," *Yale French Studies*, no. 55/56 (1977), 143.

32. Ibid., p. 107.

33. *The Anxiety of Influence*, p. 61.

34. *The Development of Abstractionism*, p. 56.

Chapter II

1. Quoted by Sheila Rothman, *Woman's Proper Place* (New York: Basic Books, 1978), p. 39.

2. Katz discusses this affair in his "Introduction" to Gertrude Stein, *Fernhurst, Q.E.D., and Other Early Writings by Gertrude Stein* (New York: Liveright, 1971), pp. xxxi-xxxvi. Katz mistakenly identifies Martha Carey Thomas as Helen Carey Thomas, p. xxxi. For other accounts of the affair see: Bertrand Russell, *Autobiography*, Vol. I (Boston: Little Brown and Co., 1967), p. 194; and Edith Finch, *Carey Thomas of Bryn Mawr* (New York: Harper and Brothers, 1947), pp. 194-95.

3. Respectively: Kay Armatage, "Gertrude Stein, The Mother of us All," *Sixpack*, no. 5 (Fall 1973) n.p.; Catherine Stimpson, "The Mind, the Body and Gertrude Stein," *Critical Inquiry*, 3:3 (1977), 497; James Mellow, *Charmed Circle: Gertrude Stein and Company* (New York: Avon Books, 1975), pp. 88-89.

4. Kay Armatage, "Gertrude Stein and the Nineteenth-Century Women's Movement," *Room of One's Own*, 3:3 (March 1977), 29.

5. See Katz, "Introduction," p. xxxiv; Mellow, *Charmed Circle*, p. 88; and Richard Bridgman, *Gertrude Stein in Pieces* (New York: Oxford University Press, 1977), p. 46.

6. "The Value of College Education for Women," typed copy made by Barbara Pollock, in the Gertrude Stein Collection, Collection of American Literature, Yale University Library, tentatively dated 1897-98. Stein was delivering her speech in Baltimore, and says: "There is nothing more striking . . . to a person who has come from the North to the South than the complete difference in the ideals and occupations in the two places." She also notes that for women in the Northeast it is a "duty" to take special care about, and interest in their children's education, while apparently this is not the case in the South.

7. Rothman, *Woman's Proper Place*, especially pp. 39-42, and Chapter 3, "Ideology and Educated Motherhood."

8. Charlotte Perkins Gilman, *Women and Economics: A Study of the Economic Relation Between Men and Women as a Factor in Social Evolution*, ed. Carl N. Degler (New York: Harper and Row, 1966), pp. 31-32.

9. Stein, "The Value of College Education for Women."

10. Finch, *Carey Thomas of Bryn Mawr*, p. 194.

11. Stein, *Fernhurst, Q.E.D., and Other Early Writings by Gertrude Stein* (New York: Liveright, 1971), p. 7. All citations are to this edition and will hereafter be included in parentheses in the text.

12. For an interesting discussion of Stein's anomalous sexual position and the conflicts this gave rise to, see Stimpson, "The Mind, the Body, and Gertrude Stein."

13. Katz, "Introduction," p. xxxii.

14. Ibid., p. xxxiv.

15. Bridgman, *Gertrude Stein in Pieces*, p. 46.

16. Leo Bersani, *A Future for Astyanax: Character and Desire in Literature* (Boston: Little Brown and Co., 1976), p. 63.

Chapter III

1. Letter from Robert Merrill Co. to Mabel Weeks, November 14, 1907, in the Gertrude Stein Collection of American Literature, Yale University Library.

2. Quoted by James R. Mellow, *Charmed Circle: Gertrude Stein and Company* (New York: Avon Books, 1974), p. 160.

3. Gertrude Stein, *Three Lives*, Vintage edition (New York: Random House, no date, but 1936 copyright renewal), p. 233. All citations are to this edition, and hereafter the page number will be given in parentheses in the text.

4. "The Storyteller," *Illuminations*, ed. Hannah Arendt (New York: Harcourt, Brace and World, 1968), p. 99.

5. Quoted by John Brinnin, *The Third Rose: Gertrude Stein and Her World* (Boston: Little, Brown and Co., 1959), p. 122.

6. Ibid., p. 121.

7. "Gertrude Stein Talking—A Transatlantic Interview," *A Primer for the Gradual Understanding of Gertrude Stein*, ed. Robert Bartlett Haas (Santa Barbara, Calif.: Black Sparrow Press, 1976), p. 15.

8. Ibid., p. 15.

9. Brinnin, *The Third Rose*, pp. 136-51.

10. Mellow, *Charmed Circle*, p. 94.

11. Janet Hobbehouse, *Everybody Who Was Anybody: A Biography of Gertrude Stein* (New York: G.P. Putnam's Sons), p. 72.

12. Lucille M. Golson, "The Michael Steins of San Francisco: Art Patrons and Collectors," *Four Americans in Paris: The Collections of Gertrude Stein and Her Family* (New York: The Museum of Modern Art, 1970), p. 43.

13. Mellow, *Charmed Circle*, p. 157.

14. *The Autobiography of Alice B. Toklas* (New York: Vintage Books, 1960), p. 34, is the first place Stein mentions Flaubert's influence. Defenses against surrealism are scattered throughout the *Autobiography*; another instance is Alice's claim that "Gertrude never had subconscious reactions...." p. 79.

15. Quoted by Alan Spiegel, *Fiction and the Camera Eye* (Charlottesville: University Press of Virginia, 1976), p. 18.

16. Ibid., p. 30.

17. Gustave Flaubert, *Three Tales*, trans. Robert Baldick (Baltimore, Md.: Penguin Books Inc., 1969), pp. 30-31.

18. Spiegal, *Fiction and the Camera Eye*, p. 29.

19. Gertrude Stein, *Fernhurst, Q.E.D., and Other Early Writings by Gertrude Stein* (New York: Liveright, 1971), p. 76.

20. J. Laplanche and J.-B. Pontalis, *The Language of Psycho-Analysis*, trans. Donald Nicholson-Smith (New York: W. W. Norton and Co., 1973), p. 78.

21. Ibid., p. 98.

22. For a convincing discussion of this point, see Peter Brooks, "Freud's Masterplot: *Questions of Narrative" Yale French Studies*, no. 55/56 (1977), 280-300.

23. "The Storyteller," *Illuminations*, p. 94.

24. Ibid., pp. 100-101.

25. Brooks, "Freud's Masterplot," 289.

26. Sigmund Freud, "Thoughts for the Times on War and Death," *The Standard Edition of the Complete Psychological Works of Sigmund Freud*, ed. James Strachey (London: The Hogarth Press, 1978), Vol. 14, p. 291.

27. In her lecture "Portraits and Repetition," Stein says, "It is the element of remembering that makes novels so soothing." See *Gertrude Stein: Writings and Lectures 1909-45*, ed. Patricia Meyerowitz (Baltimore, Md.: Penguin Books, 1971), pp. 99-124.

Chapter IV

1. The two other great twentieth-century books according to Stein were *Ulysses* and *Remembrance of Things Past*. Stein advertises her book in *Everybody's Autobiography* (New York: Vintage Books, 1973), p. 99.

2. Dianne F. Sadoff, "Storytelling and the Figure of the Father in *Little Dorrit," PMLA*, 95:2 (March 1980), 234.

3. Edward Said, *Beginnings: Intention and Method* (New York: Basic Books, Inc., 1975), p. 146.

4. Ibid., p. 163.

5. Roland Barthes, *The Pleasure of the Text*, trans. Richard Miller (New York: Hill and Wang, 1975), p. 47.

6. David Carroll, "For Example: Psychoanalysis or the Conflict of Generation(s)," *Sub-Stance*, no. 21 (1978), 53.

7. Sandra M. Gilbert and Susan Gubar, *The Madwoman in the Attic: The Woman Writer and the Nineteenth-Century Literary Imagination* (New Haven: Yale University Press, 1979), p. 49.

8. Leon Katz talks about his discovery of this fragment and places the time of its writing in his "Introduction," to Gertrude Stein, *Fern-*

hurst, Q.E.D., and Other Early Writings by Gertrude Stein (New York: Liveright, 1971).

9. Gertrude Stein, *The Making of Americans* (1903 fragment), Stein, *Fernhurst, Q.E.D., and Other Early Writings*, pp. 137, 145.

10. Ibid., p. 152.

11. Ibid., p. 155.

12. Ibid., p. 156.

13. Ibid., p. 157.

14. Ibid., p. 163.

15. Ibid., p. 147.

16. Ibid., p. 162.

17. Ibid., p. 138.

18. Ibid., p. 170.

19. Gilbert and Gubar, *The Madwoman in the Attic*, p. 14.

20. Gertrude Stein, *The Making of Americans: Being a History of a Family's Progress* (New York: Something Else Press, 1966), pp. 489-90. All citations are to this edition and hereafter the page number will be given in parentheses in the text.

21. Michel Foucault, *Power, Truth, Strategy*, ed. Meaghan Morris and Paul Patton (Sydney, Australia: Feral Publications, 1979), p. 36.

22. Stein refers to this lecture in a freshman theme of April 25, 1895; see Rosalind Miller, *Form and Intelligibility* (New York: Exposition Press, 1949), p. 146. See also "Portraits and Repetition," *Gertrude Stein: Writings and Lectures 1909-45*, ed. Patricia Meyerowitz (Baltimore, Md.: Penguin Books, 1967), p. 101.

23. William James, "The Will to Believe," *The Will to Believe and Other Essays in Popular Philosophy* (New York: Dover, 1956), p. 2.

24. Gertrude Stein's description of *The Making of Americans*, in *Everybody's Autobiography*, (New York: Vintage Books, 1973), p. 138.

25. Stein wrote this in a Radcliffe theme dated December 20, 1894; see Miller, *Form and Intelligibility*, p. 122.

26. Richard Bridgman, *Gertrude Stein in Pieces* (New York: Oxford University Press, 1970), pp. 66-67.

27. H. Marshall Leicester, Jr., "The Art of Impersonation," *PMLA* 95:2 (March 1980), 217.

28. Ibid., p. 217.

29. Wendy Steiner, *Exact Resemblance to Exact Resemblance: The Literary Portraiture of Gertrude Stein* (New Haven: Yale University Press, 1978), p. 8.

30. John Wild, *The Radical Empiricism of William James* (New York: Doubleday and Co., Inc., 1969), p. 106.

31. "Cultivated Motor Automatism: A Study of Character in Relation to Attention," *Psychological Review* (May 1898).

32. Steiner points out that "terms like 'independent' and 'dependent' had not only psychological but also spatial and grammatical value for Stein" and reproduces a "sentence diagram" from Stein's notebooks in *Exact Resemblance to Exact Resemblance*, pp. 137-38.

33. Ortega y Gasset, "History as a System," *History as a System and Other Essays Toward a Philosophy of History* (New York: W. W. Norton and Co., 1961), pp. 215-16.

34. J. Laplanche and J.-B. Pontalis define Abraham's concept in *The Language of Psycho-Analysis*, trans. Donald Nicholson-Smith (New York: W. W. Norton and Co., 1973), p. 35.

35. Ibid., p. 35.

36. Ibid., pp. 34-36.

37. Quoted by Thomas Fries, "The Impossible Object: The Feminine, the Narrative (Laclo's *Liaisons Dangereuses* and Kleist's *Marquise Von O* . . .)," *MLN*, 91 (1976), 1305.

38. Ibid., p. 1313.

39. Michel Foucault, "The Discourse on Language," *The Archaeology of Knowledge*, trans. A. M. Sheridan Smith (New York: Pantheon Books, 1972), p. 216.

40. I am referring here to Jacques Derrida's play on the double sense of "supplement" which can mean either to supply a deficiency or to supply something additional. "Whether it adds to or substitutes itself, the supplement is exterior, outside of the positivity to which it is super-added, alien to that which, in order to be replaced by it, must be other than it." *Of Grammatology*, trans. Gayatri Spivak (Baltimore, Md.: The Johns Hopkins University Press, 1976), p. 145.

41. *L'Entretien Infin* (Paris: Gallimard, 1969), p. 503. I am grateful to Larysa Mykyta for pointing out this essay and translating it for me.

42. Gertrude Stein, "Composition as Explanation," *Writings and Lectures*, p. 25.

43. John Wild, *The Radical Empiricism of William James*, p. 60.

44. In her notebooks Stein wrote "Aesthetic is the whole of me." Quoted by Leon Katz, "The First Making of *The Making of Americans*," Diss. Columbia University 1963, p. 95.

45. Ibid., p. 81.

46. "The Gradual Making of *The Making of Americans*," *Writings and Lectures*, p. 96.

47. Ibid., p. 96.

48. Said, *Beginnings*, p. 162.

49. Mark Spilka, "Turning the Freudian Screw," an essay in the Norton Critical Edition of Henry James, *The Turn of the Screw*, ed. Robert Kimbrough (New York: W. W. Norton & Co., 1966), p. 250.

50. G. A. Starr, *Defoe and Spiritual Autobiography* (Princeton: Princeton University Press, 1965), pp. 6, 12.

51. "The Gradual Making of *The Making of Americans*," pp. 89-91.

52. *Writing Degree Zero*, trans. Annette Lavers and Colin Smith (Boston: Beacon Press, 1967), pp. 30-31, 33.

53. *S/Z*, trans. Richard Miller (New York: Hill and Wang, 1974), p. 76.

54. Gertrude Stein, "Gertrude Stein Talking—A Transatlantic Interview," *A Primer for the Gradual Understanding of Gertrude Stein*, ed. Robert Bartlett Haas (Santa Barbara, Calif.: Black Sparrow Press, 1976), p. 17.

55. Ibid., p. 17.

56. I would like to thank Dianne Hunter for pointing out that the present participle is very much evident in German immigrant speech patterns.

57. "Portraits and Repetition," *Writings and Lectures*, p. 105.

58. "What Are Masterpieces and Why There Are So Few of Them," *Writings and Lectures*, p. 149, p. 153.

59. Ibid., p. 152.

60. Stein made this remark in a lecture given at Oxford in 1926. See James R. Mellow, *Charmed Circle: Gertrude Stein and Co.* (New York: Avon Books, 1974), pp. 354-55.

61. Bridgman, *Gertrude Stein in Pieces*, p. 86.

62. "What Are Masterpieces," p. 156.

63. Stein was recalling her experience of ending *The Making of Americans* in *Everybody's Autobiography* (New York: Vintage Books, 1973), p. 266.

64. Gertrude Stein, *Picasso* (London: B. T. Baleford, Ltd., 1938), p. 49.

65. *Tender Buttons*, in *Writings and Lectures*, p. 195.

Index

About the Author

JANICE L. DOANE is Assistant Professor of English at St. Mary's College, Moraga, California. Her articles have appeared in *Gender Studies: New Approaches to Feminist Criticism, Enclitic, Studies in American Fiction,* and *Salmagundi.*

Selected Bibliography

Armatage, Kay. "Gertrude Stein and the Nineteenth-Century Women's Movement." *Room of One's Own,* 3:3 (March 1977), 28-36.

———. "Gertrude Stein, The Mother of Us All." *Sixpack,* no. 5 (Fall 1973), n.p.

Barthes, Roland. *The Pleasure of the Text.* Trans. Richard Miller. New York: Hill and Wang, 1975.

———. *S/Z.* Trans. Richard Miller. New York: Hill and Wang, 1974.

———. *Writing Degree Zero.* Trans. Annette Lavers and Colin Smith. Boston: Beacon Press, 1967.

Benjamin, Walter. *Illuminations.* Ed. Hannah Arendt. New York: Harcourt, Brace and World, 1968.

Bersani, Leo. *A Future for Astyanax: Character and Desire in Literature.* Boston: Little Brown and Co., 1976.

Blanchot, Maurice. "A Rose Is a Rose ... "*L'Entretien Infin.* Paris: Gallimard, 1969.

Bloom, Harold. *The Anxiety of Influence.* New York: Oxford University Press, 1970.

Bridgman, Richard. *Gertrude Stein in Pieces.* New York: Oxford University Press, 1970.

Brinnin, John Malcolm. *The Third Rose: Gertrude Stein and Her World.* Boston: Little, Brown and Company, 1959.

Carroll, David. "For Example: Psychoanalysis or the Conflict of Generation(s)." *Sub-Stance,* no. 21 (1978), 49-67.

Copeland, Carolyn Faunce. *Language and Time and Gertrude Stein.* Iowa City: University of Iowa Press, 1971.

Dante, Alighieri. *La Vita Nuova.* Trans. Mark Musa. Bloomington: Indiana University Press, 1971.

DeKoven, Marianne. *A Different Language: Gertrude Stein's Experimental Writing*. Madison: University of Wisconsin Press, 1983.

De Man, Paul. "Autobiography as De-facement." *MLN*, 94:5 (December 1979), 919-30.

Derrida, Jacques. *Of Grammatology*. Trans. Gayatri Spivak. Baltimore, Md.: Johns Hopkins University Press, 1976.

Felman, Shoshana. "Turning the Screw of Interpretation." *Yale French Studies*, no. 55/56 (1977), 94-207.

————. "Women and Madness: The Critical Phallacy." *Diacritics* 5 (Spring 1975), 2-10.

Finch Edith. *Carey Thomas of Bryn Mawr*. New York: Harper and Brothers, 1947.

Flaubert, Gustave. *Three Tales*. Trans. Robert Baldick. Middlesex, England: Penguin Books, 1969.

Foucault, Michel. "The Discourse on Language." *The Archaeology of Knowledge*. Trans. A. M. Sheridan Smith. New York: Pantheon Books, 1972.

————. *The History of Sexuality, Vol. I: An Introduction*. Trans. Robert Hurley. New York: Vintage Books, 1980.

————. *Power, Truth, Strategy*. Ed. Meaghan Morris and Paul Patton. Sydney: Feral Publications, 1979.

Freud, Sigmund. *Beyond the Pleasure Principle. The Standard Edition of the Complete Works of Sigmund Freud*. Vol. XVIII. Ed. James Strachey. London: Hogarth Press, 1958.

————. "Remembrance, Repeating and Working Through." *The Standard Edition*. Vol. XII.

————. "Thoughts for the Times on War and Death." *The Standard Edition*. Vol. XIV.

Fries, Thomas. "The Impossible Object: The Feminine, the Narrative (Laclo's *Liaisons Dangereuses* and Kleist's *Marquise Von O . . .*)." *MLN*, 91 (1979), 1296-1326.

Gallup, Donald, ed. *The Flowers of Friendship: Letters Written to Gertrude Stein*. New York: Alfred A. Knopf, 1953.

Gasset, Ortega y. *History as a System and Other Essays Toward a Philosophy of History*. New York: W. W. Norton and Co., 1961.

Gilbert, Sandra M. and Susan Gubar. *The Madwoman in the Attic: The Woman Writer and the Nineteenth-Century Literary Imagination*. New Haven: Yale University Press, 1979.

Gilman, Charlotte Perkins. *Women and Economics: A Study of the Economic Relation Between Men and Women as a Factor in Social Evolution*. Ed. Carl N. Degler. New York: Harper and Row, 1966.

Golson, Lucille M. "The Michael Steins of San Francisco: Art Patrons and Collectors." *Four Americans in Paris: The Collections of Gertrude Stein and Her Family*. New York: Exhibition at the Museum of Modern Art, 1970.

Haas, Robert Bartlett, ed. *A Primer for the Gradual Understanding of Gertrude Stein*. Santa Barbara, Calif.: Black Sparrow Press, 1976.

Hobehouse, Janet. *Everybody Who Was Anybody: A Biography of Gertrude Stein*. New York: G.P. Putnam's Sons, 1975. Philadelphia: University of Pennsylvania Press, 1966.

Hoffman, Michael. *The Development of Abstractionism in the Writings of Gertrude Stein*.

———. *Gertrude Stein*. Davis: University of California, 1976.

James, Henry. *The Wings of the Dove*. Columbus: Charles E. Merrill, 1970.

James, William. *Psychology: Briefer Course*. New York: Collier Books, 1962.

———. *The Will to Believe and Other Essays in Popular Philosophy*. New York: Dover, 1956.

Katz, Leon. "The First Making of *The Making of Americans*." Diss. Columbia University 1963.

———. "Introduction." *Fernhurst, Q.E.D. and Other Early Writings by Gertrude Stein*. New York: Liveright, 1971.

Laplanche, J. and J.-B. Pontalis. *The Language of Psycho-Analysis*. Trans. Donald Nicholson-Smith. New York: W. W. Norton and Co., 1973.

Leicester, H. Marshall. "The Art of Impersonation." *PMLA* 95:2 (March 1980), 213-24.

Mellow, James. *Charmed Circle: Gertrude Stein and Company*. New York: Avon Books, 1975.

Miller, J. Hillis. "Narrative and History." *ELH*, 41:3 (Fall 1974), 455-73.

Miller, Rosalind. *Gertrude Stein: Form and Intelligibility*. New York: Exposition Press, 1949.

Rothman, Sheila. *Woman's Proper Place*. New York: Basic Books, 1978.

Russell, Bertrand. *Autobiography, Vol. I*. Boston: Little, Brown and Company, 1967.

Sadoff, Dianne F. "Storytelling and the Figure of the Father in *Little Dorrit*." *PMLA*, 95:2 (March 1980), 234-45.

Said, Edward. *Beginnings: Intention and Method*. New York: Basic Books, Inc., 1975.

Schmitz, Neil. "Gertrude Stein as Post-Modernist: The Rhetoric of *Tender Buttons*." *Journal of Modern Literature*, 3 (July 1974), 1203-18.

————. *Huck and Alice: Humorous Writing in American Literature.* Minneapolis: University of Minnesota Press, 1983.

————. "Portrait, Patriarchy, Mythos: The Revenge of Gertrude Stein." *Salmagundi,* no. 40 (Winter 1978), 69-91.

Simon, Linda. *The Biography of Alice B. Toklas.* Garden City, N.Y.: Doubleday and Co., 1977.

Sontag, Susan. *Styles of Radical Will.* New York: Dell Publishing Co., 1969.

Starr, G. A. *Defoe and Spiritual Autobiography.* Princeton: Princeton University Press, 1965.

Stein, Gertrude. *The Autobiography of Alice B. Toklas.* New York: Random House, 1933.

————. *Bee Time Vine and Other Pieces.* New Haven: Yale University Press, 1953.

————. *Everybody's Autobiography.* New York: Vintage Books, 1937.

————. *Fernhurst, Q.E.D. and Other Early Writings.* New York: Liveright, 1971.

————. *The Geographical History of America.* New York: Random House, 1936.

————. *Geography and Plays.* New York: Something Else Press, 1968.

————. *The Making of Americans.* New York: Something Else Press, 1966.

————. *Picasso.* London: B. T. Baleford, Ltd., 1938.

————. *Three Lives.* New York: Random House, 1909.

————. *Gertrude Stein: Writing and Lectures, 1909-1945.* Ed. Patricia Meyerowitz. Baltimore Md.: Penguin Books, 1971.

Steiner, Wendy. *Exact Resemblance to Exact Resemblance: The Literary Portraiture of Gertrude Stein.* New Haven: Yale University Press, 1978.

Stewart, Allegra. *Gertrude Stein and the Present.* Cambridge: Harvard University Press, 1967.

Stewart, Samuel, ed. *Dear Sammy: Letters from Gertrude Stein.* Boston: Houghton Mifflin Co., 1977.

Stimpson, Catherine. "The Mind, the Body, and Gertrude Stein." *Critical Inquiry* 3:3 (Spring 1977), 489-506.

Toklas, Alice B. *Staying on Alone: Letters of Alice B. Toklas.* Ed. Edward Burns. New York: Liveright, 1973.

Wild, John. *The Radical Empiricism of William James.* New York: Doubleday and Co., 1969.